Endorsements for T

"Well written and well thought out which makes a sentimental and real story which I am sure readers from around the world will enjoy. A few stories in old China have also touched on some of the same issues which makes them such an enjoyment to read. You almost feel like you lived through it. Well done Pashmina."

~ *Lorraine Hahn former anchor CNN and CNBC*

"*The Cappuccino Chronicles* is a strong and passionate story about culture, family and friendship. The author, Pashmina, vividly captures the lives of four completely different women from four different perspectives while bringing them together at the same time. I recommend this book to readers who want to be moved by words. I'd just like to offer one word of caution... once you start reading this book you may not be able to put it down until you finish it!"

~ *Judy O'Beirn International Bestselling Author,* Unwavering Strength

"I am both humbled and grateful to have shared your journey in editing *The Cappuccino Chronicles*. Pashmina you have an amazing appetite for life and your energy to produce great material is limitless. Continue to inject all of yourself in every line, in every paragraph of all your books and allow the world to see your wealth of kindness."

~ *Erica Saunders, editor, Hasmark Publishing*

MAY 2017

Dear
Rebecca,
Hope you enjoy
be jours,
love,

The Cappuccino Chronicles

Pashmina P.

Published by
Hasmark Publishing, judy@hasmarkservices.com
Copyright © 2016 Pashmina P.

Second Edition, 2016
First Edition, © 2003 Written by Pashmina P.

Disclaimer

This book is designed to provide information and motivation to our readers. It is sold with the understanding that the publisher is not engaged to render any type of psychological, legal, or any other kind of professional advice. The content of each article is the sole expression and opinion of its author, and not necessarily that of the publisher. No warranties or guarantees are expressed or implied by the publisher's choice to include any of the content in this volume. Neither the publisher nor the individual author(s) shall be liable for any physical, psychological, emotional, financial, or commercial damages, including, but not limited to, special, incidental, consequential or other damages. Our views and rights are the same: You are responsible for your own choices, actions, and results.

Permission should be addressed in writing to Pashmina P. at pashmina.p.writer@gmail.com

Editor, Erica Saunders

Cover Design and Layout, Anne Karklins
annekarklins@gmail.com

ISBN-13: 978-1-988071-39-8
ISBN-10: 1988071399

Author's Note:

To all the **Annabelle Noors** out there: it only takes a little bit of letting go to release the passion.

To all the **Sophia Martins** out there: keep living in the moment.

To all the **Sharon Connells** out there: you rock.

To all the **Dave Middletons** out there: thank you for the array of colour you sprinkle into our lives.

To all the **Washington Cannellis** out there: keep believing in free will!!

To all the **Mala Amanis** out there: don't stop learning. It's fun isn't it?

To all the **Milas** out there: keep shining.

To all the **Durgas** out there: keep on showering us with your light and love.

To all the **Angels** out there: thank you. Thank you. Thank you.

To the **Universe**: you ROCK MY WORLD.

Dedications

My beautiful daughters, thank you for choosing me, you are my brightest stars. My mother, I love you, thank you for giving birth to me. My father (may his soul rest in eternal and blissful peace). My family and friends, who are a constant inspiration in my life. To Billy, my rock, thank you for being my best friend in the whole wide world! You make my heart smile and my soul giggle! Love you!

Acknowledgements

Thank you to my family for always being there for me. I love you endlessly.

Thank you to my friends near and far. You know who you are. Thank you for always being my second family and never making me feel without.

Thank you Naveed and Sonika from Naveed and Sonika Coaching and your Thinking Into Results Program *www.naveedsonika.com*

Thank you Hasmark Publishing and your amazing editing and creative team. Thank you Judy O'Beirn for our initial conversation and your knowing and feeling my excitement when you received my manuscript.

Thank you Erica Saunders, my editor, who loved reading my book, and gave me stellar advice. Thank you for showing me that age is just a number.

Thank you Sam Strozzo… my editing partner. Thank you for being on this journey with me. You really are a *Masterji*. And thank you for always making me smile at school.

Thank you Jessica Pelham. *www.peacefulhearthypnosis.com*

Thank you Willian Reis De Souza, Founder and CEO, Dharaglobal Ltd. *www.dharaglobal.com* "Where Partnerships Begin."

Sharon

Sharon, or sometimes Ms. Connell, is Ms. Sharon Connell – our 'Little One', a teacher by day and a best friend to all at all times of her life. Born in Ireland and moved to Asia when she was two, Sharon is a teacher during the day and a very conscientious and focused student at night. She worked hard to obtain her degree as a Special Needs teacher and labels herself a keen educator. Sharon's degree led her to a tiny local Chinese school in Chinatown in London.

She has the patience of a miracle and her bond with her students would be enough to make Mussolini cry. Her students and their parents adore her and always buy her little gifts to show their appreciation.

Her petite frame, sparkling green eyes and fiery red hair make her the epitome of all angels. Her view on life is direct, yet subtle. She is pragmatic, unapologetic and well loved by everyone around her. She makes friends with ease and grace, and she supports her friendships and connections with people through love, compassion and a hard dose of reality.

Her unselfish attitude towards the children and her belief in humanity make her see life in one way – through the eyes of respect. Respect for life. Respect for others, and above all else, and as she always says *"Respect for your bloody self! Goddammit!"*

Noor

Her last name is actually "Noor." Her first name is Annabelle. Annabelle Noor. A wanna be starlet who lives with one foot in the spiritual world and the other in a world of smoking, drinking, dancing and living the high life. She is beautiful and always manages to outshine everyone at any function. Her soft plush skin and dreamy eyes with 'lay me down' eyelids make her heritage, half Indian and half Russian, gleam like a beam of light. She emanates both decorum and grace.

She met Mala and Sharon on the night of a university charity function and the three soon became very good friends, at Boston University. Life then brought all three of them back to London. Together. Over the years they have developed a very sisterly friendship which has given way to some interesting conversations. She always refers to Mala and Sharon as her '*best aunties*'.

The three of them sit at their local coffee shop, Bazica, almost every day.

Fatima

Bazica, nestled behind St. Alban's Grove in the heart of Kensington is run by a Lebanese family that has lived in London for 25 years. Fatima is the second oldest daughter of a family of six sisters and three brothers. She helps her father run the coffee shop every day while her mother stays at the back of the shop – cooking and tending to their entire family including grandparents, in-laws, 'out laws,' and various other members of their 'clan.'

Fatima always wears her *burka* and frequently smiles at the three ladies with her soft, pure grey eyes. Fatima always freezes in a tableau when her father, Benjamin, is talking to one of his "*British-bird friends*." Poor Benjamin has such a thick accent, he makes Noor, Mala, and Sharon giggle with absolute delight. Fatima's mother is always in the back, heard but not seen. She often yells in the back at her three young sons to hurry up with homework so they can help their father at the front of the shop.

Mala

Here is an Indian girl born in India, grown up in California, carrying an American accent and currently living with her West Indian boyfriend in – you guessed it – Hammersmith. Mala is also a teacher at the local school down the road.

A delicate woman with the wisdom of the trees, spiritual and very sensitive, she understands the meaning of humanity, but never stays within the confines of anything, including religion, tradition, society or fast food.

She has a party animal streak in her, which is always ready to be unleashed. She believes in free will and always thanks her nine spirit guides for watching over her when she decides to go far beyond the 'free will' track. To add injury to her culture, besides always referring to her as 'aunty' even when she was in her 20s, Sharon and Noor amuse themselves by referring to Mala as a *bungy* – an Indian word for toilet cleaner.

Mala's controversial ways while blending spirituality into the fabric of her life confuse a lot of people. Although she is Indian by heritage, she is very westernised and this scares some of her real aunties who live on the other side of London

Chapter 1

London

"Oh my God! Sharon, you are really crazy! Why are you so funny?" Mala was cackling like a hyena.

Sharon had just finished berating Jeremy, Noor's boyfriend, who was a complete waste of time and energy. He had promised to meet Noor for some furniture shopping and never made it to their scheduled destination.

"He was out until nine this morning and he didn't even bother to call me once." Noor was almost in tears as she spoke.

"Did you call him?" asked Sharon.

"At seven, and he said he was already shopping for furniture," Noor said with a worried look.

Mala and Sharon were in silly fits of laughter, mocking their poor friend. Mala was giggling so much she spat coffee all over the table at Bazica. Fatima looked over with a glittery twinkle in her grey eyes, and smiled at the three friends.

Bazica – always a haven of familiar smells and spiritual traffic at various hours of the day. Nestled at the back, behind a muse, the French-looking café had spectacular floor-to-ceiling white French windows, and charming yet comfortable furniture. One might feel like being in Ibiza, Spain. The decor was simple, clean and elegant. The three best friends had their table which always had the 'reserved' sign on it. The table with four chairs was halfway inside and outside.

Above, a white and light yellow canopy hid half of the sky. Sharon chose this table when they had their first coffee together because of the ease and convenience of her smoking habits. For Mala and Noor, the table was a mélange of halfway in and halfway out. There was never a set ideal, and the feelings their location brought were of compromise. That's what their friendship was all about: adapting to each other and learning to flow..

Bazica was a breakfast hub for business men, tea time haunt for ladies of leisure, snack time hangout for students, hot spot for afternoon cappuccinos for friends, and refuge for evening munchies for people working late. Bazica was open all day, and it was a safe place, a family run business and a retreat the three best friends called their second home.

Not much had changed in the many years they had been visiting the café. It was renovated once, but never again after that. It didn't need to be. Benjamin, the owner, ran a very tight ship and ensured his family kept Bazica clean and inviting – somewhere anyone could hang their hat for a few hours, with the best coffee in town.

Bazica was Mala, Noor, and Sharon's second home. It was the place the three friends went to as their sanctuary – their respite from the everyday world, and a place they could be real and heal while conversing about every detail of their lives. On many occasions a sea of emotions would flood their table, like a Broadway musical. Scenes of laughter, joy, pain, sadness, accomplishments and friendship would always be the topic at table eight.

This was Fatima's favourite table and had been since she started working there ten years ago. The three *aunties* were indeed an extension of the Bazica family. Customers actually thought they were famous because of all the VIP treatment they received. The three friends, Benjamin and his family were indeed connected as a soul family, connected by love, warmth, great food, and many years of cappuccinos.

Sharon looked over at Noor and with a vaguely convinced look on her face inquired, "What kind of furniture do you think he was shopping for Noor? I believe it could be a for a carpet muncher."

She was giggling at her own joke. Mala interrupted as she saw tears stream down Noor's face.

"Leave him," Mala spoke over Sharon's silliness.

"I can't leave him Mala," Noor said. "We were going to buy a house together."

"*Were*, that's the key word here Noor… *were*… now stop this whining and leave him. Get a life babe, or get a real love life. This isn't love. His behaviour has nothing to do with loving you. He was out all night, didn't give a flying monkey's arse about you. He has no consideration; he is obviously sticking it somewhere else. How many more signs do you need?" Sharon was spitting her words out with rock hard truths.

"Noor, ten years down the road… not even… let's say five years down the road, can you see yourself having 'grandchildren' with him? Having a life of peace with him?" Mala asked with genuine sisterly concern.

"I don't know," Noor replied as she blew her nose into a tissue.

"Then that definitely means *NO VAY!*" Sharon retorted in her Irish-Indian accent. "Unless of course you don't mind that he goes shopping for furniture at 7 a.m. on Saturday mornings after not coming home?"

Sharon was a realist and almost never wrong. Her instincts and 'natural smack of reality' pierced the truths concerning her family, friends and students.

Suddenly, Sharon bolted up from her seat. "Oh God! What time is it?"

"It's only 3:30 p.m.; relax, it's such a beautiful day." Mala gazed outside the window, and her cheeks flushed as she spoke, "London is beautiful in July."

"I have to run," Sharon continued, as she picked up her bag. "I promised Ms. Cheung I would take Mui Mui to the park at four."

"I have to go soon too," said Noor, looking up from her tissue.

"I have so much last minute shopping to do before my cousin's wedding. What are you doing today Mala?"

Mala was still gazing out the window. "I think I am going to sit here, relax, and enjoy this glorious afternoon in *London town, before I shake my head and go*," she said in an Indian accent.

"*Okay aunty, ve vill see you later,*" said Sharon as she tried to shake her head from side to side like the classic Indian Bollywood actresses.

As both her friends left Bazica, Mala took a deep breath and soaked in the atmosphere around her. She watched the students filtering out of the nearby local college and reminisced about her days at Boston University. She smiled at the thought of all the crying sessions, mistakes and challenges she faced when she was so young. The contemplation of a birthday in a few months made her feel a little bit wiser.

The sun was beating down on the pavement and she decided to take a walk to Hyde Park through Kensington. As she got up to pay the bill, Mala saw Fatima's eyes twinkle again, and looked away.

"Benjamin, please put these three cappuccinos on my tab okay... and I'll see you tomorrow."

"Sure thing Mala," Benjamin replied with a thick Lebanese accent.

Mala looked over and waved at Fatima. "*Ciao* Fatima." She smiled and took the three empty cappuccino cups into the back for her mother to wash. Mala pondered on Fatima's life: No life, no school, no boyfriend, and only three girls – '*aunties*' – who visited her father's coffee shop every day to entertain her. Mala felt so lucky today and as she walked, she began to reminisce about her life, her family, her friendships and Washington

While Mala was pondering the meaning of her existence, Sharon was rushing like a mad bulldog to meet Mui Mui. She felt tired and hungry.

Ms. Connell, I thought you got lost," Mui Mui said to Sharon as she approached her on the street in Chinatown. It was their usual spot right outside the local kiosk run by Mr. Lee, a vibrant street with painted green, yellow and blue doors. Mr. Lee's was the bright yellow door.

As Sharon bent down to hug Mui Mui, she whispered, "Yes darling I thought I was lost for a while too, until I found you." They both were gleaming.

Mui Mui's mother, Lily Cheung, interrupted them, "Thank you so much Ms. Connell for taking time out of your weekend to spend the afternoon with my daughter, she really adores you."

Sharon was never impressed with Lily, but when she spoke, she never gave face to the feelings of what she *actually* thought of the woman standing in front of her.

"No worries, Ms. Cheung, your daughter needs to get out and see the big world sometimes. Fresh air is very good for the soul." As Sharon spoke, Lily glanced at the floor.

"Thank you Sharon," she said as she slowly raised her head to look deep into her green eyes. Sharon didn't feel sorry for Lily; she was just another high society Shanghainese woman who was always gallivanting around the city with her rich friends, drinking tea, talking about cheating husbands, and pretending that all their children were geniuses. Sharon always found her repugnant.

"Okay Ms. Cheung," Sharon interrupted her gaze. "I will speak to you later. I'll bring Mui Mui back at six." Sharon was in a hurry to get away from the situation. She pushed Mui Mui's wheelchair towards the park and embarked on a new day for the small girl with special needs.

"Off we go precious! Wow! Look at the sun! Isn't it a gorgeous day?" Sharon was speeding down the road with the wheel chair, as Mui Mui looked up at the sun like a two year old.

Sharon had been looking after Mui Mui for ten years. She believed the 30 year old Down Syndrome girl was actually her daughter in a previous life, and they were reunited in this life time to teach each other about love and patience.

On the other side of town, Noor stopped off at Harrods, grabbed a sandwich, ran up her mobile bill, and stopped off at an internet café to see if "Presto Preston" had written her another email. Preston was a sailor who had been on a U.S. aircraft carrier, 'The Kitty Hawk,' for four years. The first time they met was when Noor had decided to break up with Jeremy for the third time. Preston was a challenge as well as a breath of fresh air.

Their correspondence to each other was going to become a book one day. She promised herself that she would reach deep within herself to push this idea out to the universe. With so many things going on in her life, she wasn't sure where she was heading half the time. All she needed was a goal, a shift, or something to help her realise her true potential. At her age, Noor was already feeling old. She knew she had accomplished a tremendous amount in her life, but her destination was never clear.

She was a social butterfly who travelled to Paris and Venice often. She believed one thing: that her travels were part of a metamorphosis. Being away from London gave her some time to think, stretch and exhale. The only thing that bothered her was herself. She hated making decisions.

No email from Preston. She picked up the phone to call Mala. No answer. She dialed Sharon, but no answer. She looked at her mobile phone with trepidation, sighed, and dialed Jeremy's number.

"Hello?"

"Heyyyy, Annabella Bella, where are you?" Jeremy sounded so tired and hungover.

"I'm shopping, Jeremy."

"I asked where you were, not what are you doing."

"I'm at a café," Noor somberly replied.

"With who?" Jeremy inquired.

"Myself."

"Mmmmmmm…" Jeremy grunted as he rolled over in bed. He looked down at himself and realised he had no clothes on. He rolled over again, with a grin on his face and then a half smirk, and asked, "So when are you coming home Bella?"

Noor's face crumpled into disgust. "Jeremy we need to talk…"

He interrupted. "I know, I know. I should have called. I am so sorry. I was out with the guys. And I got a bit drunk. And a little high, and I got a bit carried away… you know, the usual… when I hang out with the boys. You have to trust me babe. I'm so sorry. I won't do it again. I promise. I never ever meant to hurt you and…"

Noor interrupted. "Okay Jeremy. When you have some time we really need to talk about a few things."

Jeremy had no inclination about empathy or intuition. He smiled as he looked down at his naked body and asked with the same half smirking smile. "So, you coming over soon Anabella Bella?"

"I'll call you later Jeremy."

"Cool, cool, give me a shout my booty baby… see you soon." He put the phone down and rolled back over in bed and fell asleep.

"Eeeeeeeeeeewwwwwww!!!" Noor whispered into the phone. If only she could have said it louder so the universe would pull her out of Jeremy's snake pit. 'What a freak,' she thought to herself.

As she sat, staring at the 3,020 emails she and Preston had been writing to each other for over four years, she wondered to herself if she was the freak for putting up with such an insensitive, boring, ungrateful, prat like Jeremy.

Chapter 2

South East Asia

On the other side of the world, Sophia Martin was getting ready to leave Hong Kong. She had had enough of the traffic, pollution, limited space and absolute hustle and bustle of this Asian city. She knew it was time to go. She had been planning to leave the small cramped place she called home for over seven years, but she had never made a decision.

Today was the day she was going to tell everyone she was ready to go.

She was attached to her tiny flat which was bequeathed to her by a very rich uncle, born and raised in Asia. He tragically passed away three years ago, and thereafter she moved into the flat. Uncle Peter, she considered, was indeed the 'Asian-side' of her.

Her brother and her two adorable feline babies – Max and Josie – were on her mind.

Sophia had her fair share of psychos, pimps, gangsters and stalkers in her lifetime. She believed there was absolutely no reason to have many friends or new friends because one didn't know exactly what they were getting themselves into. She was her own best friend, and enjoyed her own company. She despised the word hermit; after all, she did socialize on occasion and had a very small selected network of people she trusted.

Today she was feeling a bit lonely. She wanted to escape and find a handsome British man who could take care of her. She was tired of always looking after everyone else.

Her time in Hong Kong was a result of an expatriate package she obtained from *Bloomberg* (Asia Division). Asked to renew her contract a horrendous number of times within the last seven years, Sophia had begun to reflect on her life and the number of society's blemishes presented right in front of her very eyes.

She sat in her living room staring at the eighth contract. There was no time to brood over this matter deeply. She had already made her decision, and now she had to follow through, instead of contemplating her next move. Sophia sighed, and clicked on the VCR to watch *Inspector Morse* for the third time that week.

Chapter 3

London

After her long walk, Mala decided to stop off at Bayswater to pick up a few Indian spices from the 'Indian Provisions Store.'

"Hi Ali."

"*Ey Mala Amani – Ve hawen't seen you in so long Beti,*" Ali said as he came out of his store wiping his hands on his apron. Ali was the owner and adored Mala since the day he met her, when she first came in sheepishly to ask for cumin. Ali wanted his son Sanjay to marry this beautiful girl.

Mala loved the attention and it was on days like these she loved being Indian. Ali made it seem so carefree.

"How are you Ali?" Mala asked as she squeezed Ali's hands in a double handshake across the store counter.

"*I'm good, I'm good. Vot can I help you with today?*" Ali said in his very thick Bengali accent.

"I want to make chicken *makanvala*, should I use *garam masala*?"

"*Yes, and some jeera, fota, and maybe some cumin,*" Ali said this all at once, while shuffling around his miniscule store with his rather large belly getting in the way. Mala giggled inwardly at the sight of this.

As he placed all the spices on the counter, he picked up each bottle, wiping off a little bit of dust on the plastic packaging.

He looked up at Mala and asked, "*You really know how to cook Indian khana or vot?*"

"Of course I can cook Indian food Ali," Mala said with a very coy smile.

"*Hahahahaha!*" Ali shook his head from side to side as his laughter brightened up the store. His face was like a full moon. He looked up again from his dusting of the spice bottles and asked, "*Vot about Am-rrrrrican khana?*"

"Yes I can. I love American khana too."

Ali looked up at Mala again and whispered while rubbing his gigantic belly, "*My Sanjay really loves Am-rrrrrrican khana. I told him if he doesn't find a nice lady soon… he will become a moti like his father.*"

Mala laughed, knowing that the conversation would lead to why she wasn't married. Mala snapped out of the past and looked lovingly at Ali. "Thank you so much Ali, I'll see you soon." She picked up her spices, waved, and smiled the biggest smile ever. As she walked away she could see Ali, waving like a big brown smiling moon in her direction.

As the sun set, Mala decided she was going to have an Indian Night with her girls. As she walked out of Motis Indian Provisions Store, a stunning Indian lady walked in; she reminded Mala of her mother.

Mala took the train to Hammersmith and walked briskly to her flat. She was so excited to tell her *aunties* about her day and her plans to make them Indian *khana*.

She walked into her haven and a sensual wave of vanilla and patchouli incense found her senses. She loved her flat and loved sharing it with Washington, who wasn't home. She proceeded with her ritual of switching on the lamp by the door and turning on the corner light in her bedroom. Thanks to Noor, she believed in the serenity of *Feng Shui* and always let the 'spiritual' and 'love' corners of her house glow with an abundance of light. Noor had helped her decorate her flat in Hammersmith and she made sure that the essential corners were fully lit.

Mala picked up the phone and called Sharon. No answer. It was 6:45 p.m., she wondered if Sharon was still with Mui Mui. She dialled Noor.

"*Heyyy vot you doing auntyji?*"

"Hey Mala." Noor sighed.

"What's up *auntyji?*" Mala asked with concern.

"I am so irritated with Jeremy." She was gritting her teeth as she spoke.

"Don't think about him Noor," Mala responded. "Just come over; I'm making Indian food tonight. Washington isn't home. We can have an *aunty* night."

"Really?" Noor was still sighing.

"Well, you know where I am if you get hungry or bored, or if you just want to leave your zone, you know where to find aunty Mala."

"I'll see how I feel, I might come over later. I just got home. I need to shower and get organised," Noor said as she began to run a bubble bath.

"Okay, suit yourself. I'm here if you need me." Mala was still happy from the day's events and smiled as she spoke approvingly into the phone. "Love you, call me later." Mala hung up.

She knew Noor was not coming over. Her friend sounded tired and fed up. She also knew Noor was the only person to blame; after all, she was responsible for her life choices. Mala was on a mission tonight to make Indian chicken. She went into the kitchen, turned on the radio and started cooking up a stormy feast.

Time seemed to fly by; she glanced at her watch and saw it was already 9 p.m. Still no sign of Noor or Sharon. Mala did not want to get sensitive and decided to indulge in her 'Indian Night' alone. She switched on the TV and *Indiana Jones and the Temple of Doom* was on. She ate to her delight and watched the whole movie, while the entire time thinking about her mother.

cℐℴ

Eleven fifteen, still no sign of the girls. Mala decided to clean up. Washington's instruments were all over the living room floor and a tape labelled 'Krystyna 1995' written on the front laid amongst the pile. She opened it and hesitantly played it. She had never listened to the tape before but remembered Krystyna very clearly and distinctly.

She was a clairvoyant Mala met a long time ago and all she could recall was the distinctive vibration of her Eastern European voice. Mala remembered that after the healing with Krystyna she cried for days. She looked in the mirror and wondered what could go wrong; her day had been full of joy and she was pleasingly full.

As she listened to Krystyna's voice, she became a bit weary of some of the things she might hear. Mala believed in a higher being but she was sometimes skeptical of clairvoyants, fortune tellers, and people who claimed to know the future.

The tape began:

"You will be going through some changes. What you must remember is that you are here, in this lifetime to love, teach, and heal."

Mala smiled. Of course there would be change. Change is inevitable. 'Duh,' she thought.

"To ensure you work at your optimum level, you should imagine yourself surrounded by a yellow light, with a green light traveling through your body. Yellow symbolizes intellect and green is for healing."

Mala paused. She wasn't feeling this colour energy Krystyna was describing. The tape played for another twenty minutes. Krystyna spoke about numerology and colours, and how these concepts would play a very significant role in her life. Nothing that Mala didn't know already. She was around children all day as a teacher, and by association was always surrounded by numbers and colours.

Suddenly, the tone changed and Mala could hear the sound of her own voice echoing into the living room. She asked Krystyna about her mother, sister and Washington.

13

"Your boyfriend, he is a nice man. Yes, he is a very nice man. But I think he is sometimes holding you back. You have known each other for many lives, and he was actually your husband in your last life."

Mala swallowed. This was sounding creepy.

"You actually died when you were very young and left him with seven of your children. He was very heartbroken."

Mala was getting slightly terrified; she felt like she had been drawn into an unfamiliar vortex. Yet she listened to a bit more.

"I see another life. You were his mother. You were a very rich French courtesan."

There was a long pause.

"I see your mother."

Mala ran hastily to the tape recorder and switched it off. She was breathing a little bit harder. She didn't want to know anymore. A very sharp silvery shiver ran down her spine. She needed to speak to someone… anyone. As she made her way across the living room to pick up the phone, it rang. Mala was feeling a bit jumpy and a little bit creeped out.

She hesitated, and answered the phone. "Hello?"

"Hey *bungy*, it's me. What happened, why do you sound so scared?"

"Hey Sharon," Mala sighed in great relief.

"Sorry I didn't call back. I was out with Mui Mui until 6 p.m., and then her mother took us out for dinner. Can you believe the nerve of Lily? Silly cow said she wouldn't take Mui Mui out for dinner if I didn't go too. Bloody bitch! You know Mala, I wonder, sometimes, why people have children." Sharon was angry as she spoke.

"Me too," Mala said as the voice of Krystyna returned to her mind. Sharon seemed to hear the fright in her voice.

"What's wrong *aunty*, you okay? You sound like you've seen a ghost."

"I'm fine Sharon, I was just listening to a tape I found. It's from a reader I met a long time ago."

"Oh God! Here we go again. Find out anything new about yourself Mala? Anything you didn't know already?" Sharon asked with a trace of hard sarcasm in her voice.

Mala sighed. "Shall we better ourselves Sharon? Why don't we open a school together?"

"Oh God. NO! Mala."

"Why not? We can help children love, teach and heal."

Sharon was rolling her eyes on the other end of the phone. "Is this what the reader told you?"

"Sort of."

"Mala, what kind of school do you want to open?" Sharon asked as she began filing her toe nails.

"We could open an art school, a special needs school, any kind of school."

"You... Mala... in a special needs school, love? You don't have the wits, doll. You are so overly sensitive, you would cry every day. Your eye bags would be down to your tits." Sharon was laughing at her own joke again. "I guess there is no harm in dreaming my love."

"So what would we call it Sharon? Let's dream for a bit."

"*The Bungy Spastics Association*"...what do you think about that?" Sharon was giggling loudly.

"That is the meanest thing I have ever heard in my life. I can't believe you!" Mala was horrified.

"Oh come on Mala, have a little bit of fun... will you... now you think of something. Let's have a giggle together."

There was a slight pause. "Okay, you pretend to be the receptionist at the school and let's see what we can manifest together."

"Okay, here it goes Mala. Ring. Ring." Sharon was really getting into the game.

"Heloooo, *Special School*, how can we help youuu," Mala said in her most obnoxious receptionist voice.

Sharon was giggling so hard. "Crap name Mala. With the next one, think clearly, and put some feeling into it. Okay. Try again. Ring. Ring."

"Helooo, *The Aunties' Club*, how can I help you?"

"Ring. Ring." Sharon was giggling into her rings.

"Helooo, *Creative Minds*, how can I help youuu."

"Ring. Ring."

"Heloo, *S&M School*, what can I do you for?"

"S&M? Mala? Really?" Sarcastic Sharon rose again.

"Yes Sharon, it's the beginning of our names."

"So lame!" Try another one. Ring. Ring."

"Helloo, *Angels Residence for Special People*."

Helpless with laughter, Sharon wheezed on the phone and the next half an hour became a game of receptionist and company names, while each *aunty* took turns being the receptionist.

"Sharon we've been on the phone for half an hour talking crap." Mala's stomach was hurting from so much laughter. Plus, she was still full.

"Not crap *auntyji*, dream impossible dreams and discover the possibilities."

"Ooohhh, so philosophical aunty *Sharonji*." Mala smiled, and inquired, "Did you speak to Noor?"

"Ya, I spoke to her before I called you. She said she was playing with her pendulum, or herself. I'm not bloody sure. She mentioned something about consulting her pendulum about Jeremy." Sharon didn't sound impressed.

"Oh God!" Mala exclaimed.

"I know love, it's getting quite boring if you ask me."

"Maybe we should open a school together... the three of us." Mala sounded like a little girl. "We could call it SMS."

Sharon attempted another receptionist voice and sang into the phone, "Heloooo *SMS*, how can we help you? We help you come down to earth, so please leave your problems at the door and dial 888 for optional service. Hope we could be of some reality to you. Have a wonderful day. Goodbye!"

Mala was giggling again. "Sharon, this is getting too cheesy. I'm going to go."

"Okay *dah-ling*. I will call you tomorrow. Take it easy precious. Bye." Sharon, feeling altogether happy and light-hearted hung up the phone.

No matter how old they were, they knew how to have fun. The three ladies were comic relief, blood, family, friends for life, strangers and above all healers. Mala loved her friends and they always managed to bring humour into her life. She felt lucky again.

Washington came home and was exhausted. All he wanted was to crawl into bed with Mala and snuggle up to her. He loved her so much and was sometimes taken aback by how she tolerated his working hours. He smelt the aromatic wave of Indian spices as he walked into the kitchen. He grinned at the thought of his princess cooking Indian food. She was his little 'Mystery Mistress.' She hated it when he called her that, but he did it anyway. It gave him a great sense of comfort and release that Mala always had him on his toes. He hated high maintenance, loose, money-hungry women and drama queens. Mala was none of the above. He simply adored her.

Washington was too tired to eat, and decided to dream of eating the food in the morning. He went into their bedroom and quietly eased himself into their warm bed. Mala woke up but he stroked her jet black hair and she fell asleep again. He didn't want to wake her. It was already three thirty in the morning.

While most of London slept, Noor continued to play with her pendulum. She was so frustrated at everything. She was talking to herself.

'Right means yes, and left means no.'

She tried to hold the pendulum steady but all the answers she asked were not coming out the way she wanted. Noor felt like crying. She wondered why she hadn't gone with her father to Paris when he asked her. Tears flowed silently and suddenly she started to sob uncontrollably. With no grip on her life, Noor felt like she wanted to jump out a window.

Her thoughts started to race: Jeremy is a twat, her plans of buying a house were gone; her only cousin was getting married; no email from Preston in eight days and now, she was left with no direction. Again.

She was frustrated, and knew she had to make a decision. Her head was pounding and the vein in the middle of her head felt like a canal of fear, worry and pain. She recalled a sentence from *Friendship with God* by Neale Donald Walsh: 'I have to recreate myself anew in the next grandest vision I ever held about myself.'

She had stopped reading the book two months ago because it was too profound and made her confused. Lately, she had been feeling like there was no God and she was constantly bumping into a wall. She wanted to scream. She looked at the clock. It was already 4:15 a.m. She was shocked. She had been playing with the pendulum for over eight hours! She started to cry again. She was worried about herself. Time was flying, whizzing by, and she had no indication of any life plan. She asked herself if she was crazy.

Mala and Sharon surfaced her thoughts and a comfortable feeling of normality settled inside her. Who was she kidding, her closest friends were crazier than her. She paused and thought for a little while. And then she realised, 'They are not crazy.' Not the same way she felt in her life right now. Mala and Sharon were way ahead of her. They seemed to have plans, dreams, and most of all they made their own money. They owned their independence. Noor felt depressed again. She needed to travel, to get way from London and exhale.

Chapter 4

South East Asia

Sophia was not in the mood for the company's mandatory Monday morning meeting at 9:30 a.m. She considered it a waste of time and energy. She hated the sheer drudgery of sitting in the same chair and looking at the same mundane faces every week.

"Sophia, love, had a good weekend?" asked Gary, Sophia's boss. He was a complete waste of space and he knew it. He was chauvinistic, rude, loud and thought he was the epitome of being white, or gweilo. "What'd you get up to? Anything special?"

Sophia paused and thought for a moment. She was trying to concoct a more vivid story for Gary. Last week, at the meeting, Gary was blushing after Sophia told him she had a fantastic weekend down in Lan Kwai Fong with scores of American sailors who were in town for the weekend. After sharing several drinks with the boys she went down to 'My Friends' – a local diner and dance joint in Wan Chai – and hung out at a local pub till dawn. Oh, she also told him that it didn't end there; she had to be dragged out of 'Pineapples' – a horrible after-hours strip joint that served breakfast and pizza. She decided not to give him another semi heart attack (or hard-on) with her totally fabricated story, and settled on telling him the truth.

"I cleaned my house, thought about the higher meaning of life and watched four episodes of *Inspector Morse*."

Gary was in fits of laughter. "You are such a hoot Sophia – come on now, tell us the truth. Visit the old Wan Chai district again did we?" Gary was winking.

'What a complete tit,' Sophia thought. Hong Kong was creeping up to her and she felt like the demons were being unleashed. She hated it more and more every day.

During the meeting, she drifted off thinking about her weekend. Her brother Alister made her smile. He played in a band with all his old school friends. Alister and Sophia started living together after their Uncle Peter passed away. When Sophia's mother moved to Australia with another man, Sophia rescued her brother from a sudden depression. She moved to Asia to be close to him. The older she got, the more Sophia realised the importance of family. Alister loved his sister, but like many other siblings, sometimes took advantage of her sincere generosity.

He played in a band, and Sophia never missed any of his performances and encouraged him all the time, believing that he was going to be famous one day. She was his financial support, although it was somewhat easy for Sophia because they didn't have to pay rent, living in their uncle's flat in the heart of the city. She didn't mind doing anything and everything for him. He had been through a traumatic time when their parents divorced. He was depressed for so long, but day by day he was getting better. Sophia wanted to see him excel. She ultimately knew that she wasn't affected by her parents because she was much stronger than her brother.

The mundane morning meeting snapped her back into reality when Gary announced, "This year's Christmas party will be at the end of November, since so many people are going home for the holidays." Sophia envisioned more of a Halloween party. Gary was such a twit.

Sophia had a deep urge to call her father to tell him she was returning to London. She started smiling. The festive season was approaching and she didn't want to stay in Hong Kong for another Christmas. Last year was so plastic and plain, not to mention lonely. She spent Christmas Day at Alister's girlfriend's house – actually the house is Alister's girlfriend's parent's house, in Repulse Bay. The view was spectacular, but the company was tiresome. Alister's girlfriend, Tanya, was a rich, pampered girl who went to an English School Foundation in Hong Kong. Her parents had moved from Madrid when she was eleven years old. Sophia always referred to these kinds of children as 'spoilt expat brats.' She wondered if South East Asia was making her bitter.

Gary's loud voice interrupted her. "So, Sophia, what are you going to get us for Christmas this year?" He was gazing perversely at her.

She wanted to say, 'my resignation,' but decided to hold off on the notion and the action for a few days. She decided to tease Gary.

"Well, Gary, it really depends if you've been 'naughty or nice.'"

"You are such a spark plug. We need more of you mixed breed women around here." Gary was grinning at his unethical comment.

He really reminded her of a troll and one of the *Twits* from Roald Dahl's book. Sophia got up to leave the conference room, ignoring Gary's racist as well as sexist comment. It was already 11:30 a.m.; for the life of her, she couldn't remember what the meeting was about. She was in a different frame of mind. She went back to her desk and clicked on her computer – twenty seven new emails. It was going to be a very long day. Before she began replying to her clients, she picked up the phone and called her best friend Dave, a very reputable fashion designer for *Christian Dior* (Asia Division). He was her EVERYTHING. Alas, they could never be together because he was gay. She met him the first week she was in Hong Kong. He made her smile all the time, and supplied her with a very lighthearted view of the city's evils.

Dave answered the phone in the chirpiest voice. He sounded like a bird. "Hello my darling Sophia. How was your weekend? I didn't hear from you."

"I was contemplating life," Sophia said, as she scanned her emails

"So what's the verdict? What did you find during contemplation?"

"I'm leaving Asia."

21

"What? Really? What about me?" Dave was pretending to cry on the phone. "Seriously though, why are you leaving? This place wouldn't be the same without you."

"I know… so many people would miss me Dave." Sophia was rolling her eyes.

"Please Sophia, I can hear your eyes rolling so far at the back of your head, I can hear your eye balls gurgling in their tear ducts… and it's Monday morning, do we have to get into the mundane details of your sorry, boring, pathetic life? And what are you going to tell Gazzer?"

"I haven't told anyone yet. Just you Dave."

"And Alister?" He inquired.

"He doesn't know yet." Sophia sounded worried.

"Ooow you can leave him with me. I'll take care of him." Dave was smiling; he had a huge crush on Alister.

"Yuck Dave! Please stop perving over my brother. And I don't want him to know anything yet. I have to think about how I can tell him without hurting his feelings."

"Sophia, just say… you have decided to do something for yourself. You love him. Hope he becomes famous. And you will see him soon." Dave was also beginning to scan his emails.

"You know I can't do that."

"Don't be emotional Sophia. Sometimes we come to a point in our lives where we just have to be selfish for ourselves."

"So, I should just be horrible and inconsiderate?" Sophia was annoyed.

Dave paused. "I don't think telling someone the truth is being horrible or inconsiderate. He will understand, he is your brother for God's sake."

Sophia was perplexed. "Can we meet for a quick coffee after work?"

"Sure, so we can discuss your drama in more detail."

"You really think I'm a drama queen don't you?'

"Yes all the time Sophia."

"Thanks Dave."

"You're most welcome, Sophia, oh beautiful, graceful one... with the strength of a NOODLE!"

Sophia was smiling again. "I'm going now, see you after work."

"Okay sunshine, I'll see you later. Try not to think too much, or you might end up on Prozac like me." Dave was searching his drawer for his antidepressant.

"Bye Dave."

"Bye Noodle!"

Sophia loved Dave and he always brought her back down to earth. He was an emotional basket case, but he was true to himself, which made Sophia admire the pants off him. Her prospect of Monday didn't seem so bad after all. She was excited to meet Dave and discuss her future with him in more detail. He was the only one she could turn to right now.

Chapter 5

London

Sharon felt amazing this morning, which was unusual for her, first thing on a Monday morning. Her Sunday was extremely relaxing and she needed the rest. She slept in and decided to join her mother for a late lunch before dropping Sandy to her weekly AA meeting. This was her regular Sunday outing.

Today, she had so much to give. Sunday had energized her. Monday went by slowly, except for an accident a little boy had in her classroom. At 3:30 p.m. she looked at her watch; she was supposed to call Mala. Noor had something important she wanted to tell them. She dialled Mala.

"Hey *bungy*, Noor has something to tell us." Sharon was wiping up the floor of her classroom as she spoke.

"Oh no, is she pregnant again?" Mala asked.

"I bloody well hope not." Sharon was sickened at the urine she was mopping up.

"What time are we meeting?"

"In about half an hour love." Sharon was heaving her little body up to standing position. She sighed loudly. "I might be running a bit late. I have to clean up my bloody classroom. One of my students, bless him, pissed all over the floor today and thought he was in a bloody swimming pool. The poor gyte was doing the bloody breast stroke in his own urine… Bloody patience…"

As Sharon was telling her the mundane details of cleaning up and using Dettol, Noor was already sitting at Bazica with three cappuccinos, waiting for her friends. When Mala and Sharon finally arrived, they could see that Noor had been crying again.

"Why the long face precious?" Sharon inquired before lighting her cigarette and sitting in her usual spot.

"I have something to tell both of you," Noor said with a very tired look on her face.

"Are you pregnant? Because you are too old. You will be popping out grandkids. Did Jeremy hurt you?" Mala was concerned for her friend.

Sharon was irritated. "Let the poor girl speak Mala, will you? … bloody hell…"

Noor sighed, a heavy sigh that made her snort from her nose. "I am leaving London."

"For good?" Mala sounded shocked.

"No, not too long, six months maybe a year?"

"Why?" Sharon sounded serious and confused.

"I don't feel like I am getting anywhere here. Every time I move forward, I seem to have to take several steps backwards."

"But your cousin's wedding is next month, and my birthday and then Christmas." Mala sounded like a little girl.

"So, when are you going?" Sharon was not impressed as she blew on her cappuccino, the froth spilling over the side.

"I'm leaving in a few days," Noor replied.

"Where are you going?" Mala probed, still sounding like a six year old girl.

"To Paris to help my father."

"Why don't you get a real job in London Noor? And start smelling the bloody coffee, mate, and start realising you aren't getting any younger. I think you should stop running back to daddy whenever you run out of money." Sharon was beginning to get agitated.

Noor was stunned. "Is *that* what you think of me?"

"Sometimes," Sharon continued, "you need to stop being so God damn airy fairy and start being a grown up. Do you know what really bothers me about you two? Let me tell you. You sit here and moan and groan about life when you know that it is ultimately up to you to make a difference."

Noor interrupted, "Well, I don't know when I'm coming back."

Sharon was not yet finished and she hated being interrupted. The Irish in her hated being interrupted. "Great Noor, I wish you all the best and hope you find what you are looking for and start noticing that money or a life does not fall from the sky. I also pray that you stop feeling like a victim and make sure that every step you take, and sometimes miss, is all for a BLOODY GOOD REASON! If you can't find yourself because of sheer fear – fear of mistakes, fear of decisions, fear of love, friendship and most of all commitment… then we certainly cannot help you. Nobody can. And before we forget, let us all take a moment to reflect on how fricken lucky we are and account for everything we have been blessed with."

The three women were silent. Mala was speechless. Not in a bad way. A feeling of release embodied the air. Sharon was right. Without a doubt, she knew what she was talking about.

"I have to go." Noor stood up abruptly. "I have so much packing to do and I need to call my father so he can make all the necessary arrangements for my arrival." She walked over to the counter, paid her tab for a two month supply of coffee and left. As Fatima watched her walk out of Bazica she looked like she was about to cry. Sharon and Mala sat in silence for what seemed to be like ten minutes.

Sharon broke the silence. "What the bloody hell is wrong with that girl? You try and tell someone the truth and they get so bloody sensitive. I thought friends were supposed to be honest with each other?"

"I know Sharon, but maybe she is going through something difficult right now." Mala was trying to empathise with Noor.

"Like what? For God's sake!" Sharon was getting very mad. Her face was twisted and angry. "She has EVERYTHING! She is not stuck in Israel fighting a war, or starving to death in Ethiopia, or living in a village in China with no education. It's so easy to blame the 'universe' and 'angels' when we don't get our way. She can't just stomp her feet all the time. She has to face the music. What makes her think Paris is going to be any easier? Because her father is there, and can support her, and find a rich husband for her? We should give thanks for being alive every day, and her pathetic tantrums every three or four months is getting bloody tiring and extremely routine, like a hamster on a wheel. She is becoming one of the most uninteresting people I know."

Mala was silent.

"What, Mala? You have nothing to add?"

Mala didn't want to fuel the red-head's fire any more than it was already lit. She was also a bit scared to come under attack from one of Sharon's speeches.

Sharon was instigating the situation. "Come on Mala, what's your damage? Come on, let's hear it. Let the whole world know how weak you are and how sorry you feel for yourself too!"

"I don't know what you are talking about." Mala tried not to look into her friend's green eyes. "This isn't about me Sharon."

Sharon sighed. "See, now I'm doing it too. I'm getting wrapped up in all your silly dramas when what we should be focusing on is the now. I don't want to argue with anyone. But I'm thoroughly disgruntled and I will tell Noor myself when I am ready."

Mala looked up at Sharon. "Disgruntled?" She tried to bring some humour to the situation, hoping and praying that Sharon would finish preaching.

"Yeah… you silly *bungy*… you never heard the *vord* 'disgruntled' before?" Sharon shook her head from side to side, she was getting better and better at it every day.

27

Mala managed a tepid smile. She looked over at the empty seat and a sense of loss as well as reality hit her right in the solar plexus – the yellow *chakra*.

Fatima came over to their spot and looked at Sharon with her grey eyes. "She will be back." She paused. "Because sometimes the man dies."

Sharon gazed at her with confusion, deep green eyes locking with the smokiness of Fatima's grey eyes. "What?" Sharon asked inquiringly.

"It is from an ancient Eastern saying that tells us through death there will be birth, and sometimes the man must die first to be born again." Fatima was speaking in a majestic and mystical way. She reminded Mala of a princess.

"Thanks Fatima, that was great love. I'll remember to tell Noor the next time I see her." Sharon was smiling as well as being condescending.

As Fatima walked gracefully away, Sharon began to whisper very loudly, as she leaned in to talk to Mala. "You see, even Fatima has more of a grip on R-E-A-L-I-T-Y. She comes to this uneventful coffee shop day in and day out, while her mother slogs at the back, and her fat bastard of a father chats up women on the phone all day. She's a rock if you ask me."

"A rock?" Mala sounded confused, or maybe she wasn't paying attention to the conversation anymore.

"*Bungy*, why do you keep repeating everything I say? You are ruining the moment. I am trying to tell the truth here. Bloody *bungies*! Find humour at such odd times." Sharon was calming down, as a smile began to slowly appear on her face. She continued again, after a brief pause.

"So, Mala what do you really think about all of this? Do you think: (a) Noor should be wasting her life away thinking how shit it is? Or (b) Noor should be thinking about life, how brilliant it is and how lucky we are?"

"The latter," Mala replied.

"Very educated answer." Sharon was in teacher mode as she sat back in her chair.

"Yes, educated, but try thinking that everything around you, every single day, every single minute and every single second is fricken brilliant and is all for a higher reason is not easy. Think about that Sharon. Who can do that?" Mala didn't want to start another argument, but she had to get her point across. "How can a human being be happy ALL the time?"

"They can Mala… I think about the good all the time," Sharon said convincingly, as she sat further back in her chair looking at the sky while puffing away on her Silk Cut Lights.

Mala arrived home and flopped herself on the sofa. Washington was in the kitchen cooking black beans and rice. He heard her come through the door and greeted her with a huge hug.

The house smelt like *rhaj mahal dhal* – black lentils with *garam masala*. He was using the spices. She smiled at the thought of Washington cooking.

"How are you my Mystery Mistress? My darling who is full of spices."

"What? What do you mean spices? Do I smell or something?" Mala asked as she tucked her nose into her sweaty shirt. She still smelt like perfume. She smelled both sides of her armpits just to make sure. No spicy smell. She was confused.

"My Mystery Mistress is full of surprises, like spices."

"I don't get it babe." Mala looked even more confused.

"Spices sounds like surprises, no?" Washington asked in his burly accent. He had the tendency to be ingeniously corny at times. Tonight she wasn't in the mood and didn't get his humour.

As Washington walked back into the kitchen, he sang a beautiful love song, as he stirred his pot. She thought back to the first time she met him, in the Ritz Carlton lobby lounge. He was playing the bongos with his strong dark hands, while swaying to the beats of Afro-Caribbean music. She drifted into a slow dream, and recalled each subtle moment that led to this moment.

Fifteen minutes later she awoke. Both of them had been through so much in the long years they had been together. She walked into the kitchen and wrapped her arms around him. It still felt like the first day. They fit, like a match made in heaven, 'together' in secret for what seemed like decades. Mala thought about her day at Bazica and how her life would shift without Noor.

Mala looked up at Washington and asked him, "Babe, do you think I run away from my problems all the time?" She was trusting that he would be the one to tell her the simple truth.

"No. I think you are good at facing your worries," Washington said reassuringly as he pulled her closer. "Don't over think too much, everything is going to be alright. As humans we have to be aware of the divine melody."

Mala liked that – 'the divine melody' – she wondered where he had heard that. "That's beautiful Washington. 'The divine melody.' I love it."

"I'm a musician babe, I don't like talking… I like playing." Washington wrapped his arms around Mala and sang a Portuguese love song by Tim Maia in her ear. She wanted to freeze the moment and make it last her entire lifetime.

"Hi *Pitaji*, it's me." Noor sounded very weak.

"Hello Annabelle, how are you? Have you made some decisions yet?" Her father asked.

"Yes *Pitaji*, I am coming to Paris."

"Good. Good. You have finally come to your senses. I think you will have a better time. When are you coming Anna?"

"I'll be there tomorrow dad."

"No problem, my darling. The chauffeur will pick you up. I can't wait to see you."

"Me too."

Noor hung up the phone and felt a sense of delight and bereavement all at the same time. Her father was an educated Indian man with an abundance of tradition in his heart. He wanted Noor to marry a good Indian man who had lots of money, and hopefully live in Delhi one day. The thought of that prospect always made Noor gag from the depths of her being, but she played along as much as she could. She didn't want to get cut off from his inheritance, especially at her age.

Noor's father was a contradiction in her life; as well as being her lifeline and a source of financial abundance, the relationship came with heavy strings attached.

Mr. Noor lived in Paris. He had opened up a beautiful Moroccan restaurant with his young wife Anna Maria. Noor despised her and always felt the tug of financial freedom escaping into the hands of his father's young gold digger.

Noor started to pack and realised the only person she didn't tell was Jeremy. She began to dial his number, but decided against it and called Mala instead. They talked, laughed and Mala cried with laughter and abandonment. Noor was going to miss her sweet Indian friend.

As Noor hung up the phone, she sighed deeply, feeling as if the sigh had been stuck in every organ of her body for centuries on end. Still, she felt purposeful again. She looked at her suitcase; it was overflowing. She knew she wasn't going to be back in London for a long time. Decisions seemed to haunt her again, driving the contradiction angel through her heart while the good angel tried to sashay through her soul. She retrieved her pendulum and laid it on the bed. As she stared at it, she knew one thing was for certain: she had made her choice that night – she was leaving everything and everyone in her past very far behind her.

Chapter 6

South East Asia

The week seemed to drag on and Sophia had not yet mustered the courage to tell Gary or Alister she was leaving Asia. Dave was right, she had to tell the whole world; otherwise her manifestations of leaving would never materialize.

"Sophia, can I have a word with you in my office please?" Gary poked his head out of his room as he beckoned to her.

She walked into his office and sat down. She had been there long enough to make herself comfortable in his domain.

"The contract, have you signed it yet?" Gary asked.

"I looked over the contract and…" She paused. Alister popped up into her head.

"Yes, and… what's the problem?" Is it the insurance policy? We can change it to suit your needs. I mean, to be frank Sophia, the only thing not covered is maternity, and I don't think you'll be needing that anytime soon…" He raised his bushy eyebrows "Unless you have something to tell me."

Sophia didn't even read that part of the contract.

"I do have something to tell you Gary."

"You didn't go and get yourself knocked up did you?"

"No Gary, nothing like that…"

"Then what is the issue my dear?" he asked as he leaned over his desk.

Sophia wanted to say, 'you are the biggest issue, you obese tit, and you are a reflection of what a cesspool this society is. Furthermore, your degrading attitude towards women disgusts me. I think you are nothing more than the guck you scrape from the bottom of a septic tank. Additionally, I would like to remind you that not all Australian men who come to Asia on an expat package behave the way you do. You are exasperating, mind numbing, tactless and completely misinformed.' But, once again, she decided to play it safe and said in a controlled tone, "I'll think about it."

Gary was not happy. He look defeated and frustrated. "You keep in mind that you are one of the highest paid employees here."

"It's not about the money," Sophia retorted.

"Then what is it?" Gary asked, his emotions all over the place, making rapid atoms fly around his body and suddenly reaching his face, which began to turn red.

"You'll never understand," Sophia said as she got up to leave his office.

"Fine, fine, I know it's a woman thing. Take a few days to think about it and when you're off the rag… we…"

Sophia interrupted harshly, "Gary! I get your point."

As she got up to leave Gary slumped back into his chair, put his feet on top of the desk and said, "Hey Sophia, don't take life so seriously. Humour is the key." He winked again.

Sophia thought about the difference between humour and ridiculous. Gary had so much to learn.

Back at her desk, she felt like a wimp. She called Dave – her saviour, her mental sanctuary, her best friend, her humour box, and someone she considered 'family.'

"Hello, *Christian Dior*, how can I help you?"

"Hi, would it be possible to connect me to David Graham please?" Sophia asked in her most polite voice.

"*Shertainly, hole on.*" A-Wong, his secretary, was Chinese and had just graduated from college, and was in the midst of an internship. She had been demoted to receptionist when HR figured out she couldn't draw. Indeed, she always tried her best to pronounce words in a phonetically correct manner.

Dave finally came on the phone. "Hi, David Graham, how can I help you?" He sounded so formal.

"Dave. Sophia here. I couldn't do it. I just couldn't do it Dave. Alister kept popping up in my head."

"Couldn't do what?" Dave asked as he was dressing one of his models.

"I couldn't tell Gary I was leaving. And I still haven't told Alister yet." Sophia felt miserable.

"You're useless Sophia. What exactly is holding you back?"

"I am holding myself back Dave. It's me. I have no one to blame."

"Well then, you've answered your own question. You are your own demon. I have three options for you: see a therapist so he can prescribe you with some drugs; jump off the tallest building in Hong Kong, because you are going through a slow suicide anyway by being a pansy wansy; or, come to *Christian Dior* for some retail therapy." Dave was swirling meters and meters of fabric over his model as he spoke.

Sophia was agitated. "I am serious Dave."

"So am I Sophia. I sound like a broken down tape recorder. You know what you have to do. What did I say to you on Monday?"

"Manifest positive ideas and you will reap positive benefits." Sophia sounded so bored. Like an insolent teenager. "Let's go out and have a few drinks tonight Dave. Let's get pissed."

"That's my girl! You probably need a good vomiting too. The

demons might actually come out this time. When was the last time you got shit faced anyway?"

Sophia thought back to when she was last actually tipsy. She never got drunk. She hated to lose control. "I think it was New Year's."

"You know what Sophia? You are such an old lady. It's so disturbing. You've been sitting at home and masturbating to *Inspector Morse* too much. The thought of wrinkly old John Thaw makes me want to heave." Dave was making vulgar vomiting noises.

"Dave, you are ghastly." Sophia was rolling her eyes again. "I watch him because I love his accent and the way he speaks."

"In a Pomme accent?" Dave asked trying to sound as British as the Queen. "Sophia Martin, you are turning into my *grandma-ma*. Try watching Trainspotting or BBC…"

Sophia interrupted, "I'll meet you at 9:30 at Dolce Vita."

"Too early *grandma-ma*." Dave was enjoying himself making fun of her. She couldn't help but smile. "I will see you later my sweet love iguana." Dave put down the phone and tended to his model, who looked uncomfortable, wrapped up too tightly in a gold, silky, chiffon material. She looked like a golden mummy. Dave was perplexed. That conversation with Sophia had made him lose track of his intention. He unravelled the material and started again.

Sophia now felt a sense of relief. She was excited to see Dave and was going to tell Gary on Monday to 'Sod. Off!'

Chapter 7

London

Mala was walking around her classroom cleaning up the paint splashed all over the floor. The kindergarten she worked at hired a Sri Lankan lady to clean up after her at three thirty when the bell rang, but Mala always did it on her own. She didn't ever want to leave the classroom in a mess. It was a 'face' issue, and Asians never wanted to be branded as lazy, dirty, or uncaring. True to her values, Mala always made it a point to exemplify her actions. Her mobile phone rang incessantly. She picked it up with annoyance in her voice.

"Hello?"

"I can't believe she didn't even call to say goodbye." It was Sharon and she sounded very hurt.

"Me neither." Mala sighed. She didn't want Sharon to feel bad by telling her the truth that Noor actually did pick up the phone and say bye to her. And that they had a magical bonding session reminiscing about the good old days together.

"Why did she leave without saying goodbye?" Sharon was dragging on her cigarette in the staff room as she pondered over Noor's discourtesy.

"Because you told her the truth *aunty*." Mala sighed again as she thought about her own family. She was not feeling good this Friday.

"Now here it is," Sharon continued. "We made a choice to be here on this planet we call earth, which should have been called water because there's so much 'bleedin' water here on earth… and when we come here, we choose all the necessary lessons we need to go through for our own spiritual growth. For example, I think you, Mala, came here to learn about healing. I think Noor came here to learn about trust. And I came here to learn the truth, as well as preach it."

"So, why do you think I'm here to learn about healing?"

"Just a hunch," Sharon said with an easy tone.

Mala wanted to know more. "Seriously, give me an example."

"Okay, the whole situation with your family. Wouldn't you admit that there needs to be some kind of healing?"

"I need to heal them?"

"Maybe, and vice versa."

Mala thought back to Krystyna's tape – 'green is for healing.' She wanted to suddenly know more, or at least feel more. She thought back to when she was eight years old and her mother always reminded her that 'people manifest themselves as angels in our lives to give us ideas and direction.' She also knew deep in her core that there needed to be some sort of healing process that she and her immediate family needed to go through together. She didn't want to think about it right now. She seemed to always be pushing thoughts of her ancestors away, or at least trying to keep them at bay.

Mala sighed; she didn't want to think about herself anymore. "What about Noor?"

Sharon didn't have to think too long and hard for the answer. "Trust in herself."

"And you? Oh Irish sage?" Mala inquired.

"Truth in the world my precious *bungy.*"

"How did you get so wise Sharon?"

"I'm a smart arse love. Come on now, enough of the drama, what are we doing tonight? It's Friday!"

"Let's meet at mine and then go down to Mondo." Mala sounded chirpy again.

"Done."

"Done."

"See you tonight *aunty.*" Sharon said shaking her head from side to side on the other end of the receiver.

As she finished cleaning her room, and put all the art work on the drying racks, a painting caught her eye. Her student, Jamie, painted a boy and a lady in a flower dress holding the little boy's hand. Above the lady, he had written 'mum' and beside the picture of the boy, he wrote 'me.' When she looked closely at the picture, she noticed tiny orange droplets falling from 'mum's' eyes. She wondered what orange symbolized.

Chapter 8

South East Asia

Dolce Vita was packed. All kinds of people were out: druggies, suits, CNN reporters, ATV anchors, husbands without their wives, wives without their husbands, gay boys, gay girls; it was a dynamic mix of couples including Dave and Sophia.

"I am so glad we are doing this tonight sunshine…" Dave was dressed to the nines, and he looked absolutely ravishing. Everyone was staring at this Australian hunk of a God. "And try not to be my grandma tonight, we both need to pull, get royally laid, and get embarrassingly pissed. Now, I need your undivided attention, because I need you to help me attract the boys."

David was so camp. He cat walked very elegantly to the bar and ordered two Dirty Martinis. There was no space in the bar area, and people were actually seeping onto the sidewalk. The roads were closed on each side of Lan Kwai Fong – due to an overcrowded New Year's Eve party in 1996 that went horribly wrong. So many people had been trampled on, and trampled to death. It was horrific.

Sophia and Dave stood on the sidewalk watching everyone. Dave knew everybody and at 10 – 15 minute intervals a variety of the city's high society *moghuls* came over to schmooze with Dave. He was having the time of his life. He looked like a professional West End actor. Sophia was so happy to just watch him perform. Dave knew who his real friends were; he only had one, Sophia.

His status as a fashion designer made him an overnight success in Hong Kong. Within three weeks of his arrival, Dave Graham's picture was all over the city's high society magazines including *Tattler*, *Talkies*, *BC International* and even a few local newspapers like *Apple Daily*. Dave was a star.

In most of the magazines, Sophia was always described as the 'mysterious girl' who paraded around with Dave Graham. She always managed to pose nicely. She loved riding on Dave's coat tail of Hong Kong's elite world.

She knew how important it was to look spectacular for herself, for Dave, and for the city. If she was going to leave soon, she had to depart with flair.

Sophia was shining like an iridescent shimmer of twilight on Friday night. Wearing ankle-length, electric blue capris trousers, a baby blue sweater, stilettoes and a *Louis Vuitton* bum bag strapped around her waist, Sophia looked amazing.

"You traitor Sophia! How can you splash the LV logo all over the place, when you can have *Christian Dior* all over your delightful body? I am insulted," Dave remarked playfully, as she glowed like a blue sapphire. She looked gorgeous.

Sophia felt as good as she looked. "I am not here to do your PR Dave, you have enough monkeys doing that for you already."

"Promise me, Sophia, if any of the paparazzi come near us, you will seductively throw your LV bum bag on the floor and wrap your arms around me okay?"

Sophia was laughing. "Okay Dave, I promise."

"You swear?"

"Nope," Sophia said with a cocky grin on her face.

"Why not? I think we should create some noise for the media. The Hong Kong public would love it. You wouldn't be branded as the 'mysterious' woman anymore.

Sophia felt sexy and free. She felt this overwhelming feeling of true womanhood; now all she needed was a real *functional man* beside her.

At two thirty in the morning, Sophia and Dave ended up at the Kee Club with the manager of On Pedder, the receptionist of LVMH, the son of Asia's biggest *Ferrari* dealer, the Diane Freis in-house designer, the manager of California Company Limited, and a tall Englishman called Craig. He caught the attention of Sophia and sat with her until five thirty in the morning. Dave was standing at the bar. He winked at her, and she knew it was their cue – time to go home. The night was certainly memorable.

Chapter 9

London

Washington was working late and Mala was getting ready for Sharon's arrival. She opened a Wolf Blass Shiraz and set it on the counter to breathe. It was seven and Sharon would be over within the hour. Mala stood in front of her closet. She knew almost every woman who was going out on Friday night engaged in the same ritual: she couldn't find ANYTHING to wear. She recalled her and her younger sister referring to these days as 'fish days.' The origins of where that came from was never really explained; however, it seemed to equate to being like a fish out of water… with no clothes on.

Sharon, on the other hand, was a swift dresser, and never spent hours on shopping, clothes or makeup. Her green eyes and red hair were the perfect combination of a wow factor already. She didn't need much to bamboozle anyone. While she threw on her ensemble, Sharon's aged mother, Sandy, kept her daughter company.

"Where are you going tonight doll?" Sandy inquired.

"Out mum. Going to meet Mala first."

"What about Annabelle?" Sandy asked with a shake in her voice.

"She's in Paris mum, and don't ask me what she is doing there, because I don't bloody know," Sharon said, in an irritated tone.

"*Oohh thas lovely, I bet the lass has found a handsome soldier.*" Her Irish accent gave way to a *Mrs. Doubtfire* aura.

Sandy Connell stayed with her Sharon every weekend. Like a sensible, enlightened daughter, Sharon took it upon herself, like a ritual, to drive her mother to her AA meetings every Sunday.

"What are you doing tonight mum?" Sharon inquired while staring at herself in the mirror.

"Oh, I don't know, stay in, read a book, make a cup of tea, watch *Blind Date*," Sandy said as she picked up her copy of the *Celestine Prophecy*.

Sharon kissed her mother on the forehead and jumped into her BWW and whizzed from St. John's Wood to Hammersmith. Her parent's divorce assisted in their cushy life. No wonder she had so much to give; she had everything.

Mala was still standing in front of her closet. The doorbell rang. She opened the door. Sharon looked effortlessly cool in a pair of deep-dark denim jeans splashed with small silver studs delicately placed on her ankle, a pale pink sweater, black leather boots, and a long red leather jacket. She looked sensational. Her fiery red hair and green eyes coupled with her pink and red ensemble made her look like... Cindy Lauper... a real pop star.

"Are you going to let me in *bungy*, and why aren't you dressed?" Sharon asked, as she sashayed her way into Mala's flat.

"You look lovely Sharon," Mala said as she followed her friend into the house with her dark brown eyes, gazing with admiration at her whole body, mind and soul ensemble. What a beautiful spirit. So colourful, energetic and serene all at the same time.

"And you look like a *bungy*," Sharon said as she lit a cigarette in the kitchen. Now, hurry up and get dressed!" She was also helping herself to the wine that had been left to breathe for her arrival.

"What should I wear?" Mala inquired, still standing in her towel.

"Anything Mala, no one is going to remember tomorrow, including yourself. Now hurry, before everything shuts." Sharon gulped down her wine.

"Shall we go to La Bella Luna and watch Washington play?" Mala asked.

"No! We are not groupies and that is boring. You'll see him later. Now let's go. Hurry. Or I'm leaving without you."

Mala threw on a pair of black trousers and a beige sweater. She grabbed her suede handbag and both *aunties* left the house. Sharon couldn't drive because she was already drinking, so they both jumped in a taxi and headed down to SoHo

While Mala and Sharon partied until 3 a.m., Noor sat in her father's flat. Alone. She had been in Paris for a week already and Café Des Artistes was all she had. And her father, of course.

The restaurant still had a few teething problems and Anna Maria didn't do much to help. She just sat at the entrance, like a dragon, puffing away on a cigarette every single night. She told Noor her father had told her to sit there to attract the right people to the restaurant, the kind that he was accustomed to, or better yet *preferred*.

What did that mean? People her father were 'accustomed to?' What a sham of a woman, Noor thought to herself. She was going to tell her father that Anna Maria was not good for his health, his pocket, and definitely not his restaurant. She had to wait for the perfect moment.

She was thinking about Mala and Sharon. Noor was still upset at Sharon for being so blunt, and possibly truthful, but she didn't want to admit she was missing both of them like crazy. Nor did she want to admit she felt guilty for not saying goodbye to Jeremy or Sharon.

It was almost midnight and her father and his gold digger weren't home yet. She decided to check if Preston was thinking about her. She went into the study and clicked on the computer. One new email. Her heart raced as the email popped up.

Dear Annabelle,

Pleased to know you are helping your father, I am getting ready to go back home to see my family. Christmas is coming and I need to buy presents. Have so much work to do on the ship before we head back to the West Coast.

Will write soon.

Xo,

Preston

Was that it? How boring. She wanted more, she wanted to feel loved and feel like someone was really and truly thinking about her. She thought about a conversation she had with Jeremy two weeks before she decided to run away.

She was frowning. She felt alone. She heard her father enter the living room; he was giggling and laughing with the gold digger. He sounded so happy. She sighed, and clicked on to 'Cainer.com' and looked up her horoscope. It had been ages since she checked what her birth sign was revealing in the celestial heavens. It read:

'For you and I both know that the real secret in life is not to get what you want but to want what you've got. The latter, you will be delighted to hear, is well within your power now.'

Noor now knew she desperately needed to *'recreate herself anew in the next grandest vision she ever held about herself.'*

Sunday rolled around again and Sharon was driving her mother to Sloane Square for her AA meeting. There was a comfortable silence in the car as they drove down South Kensington.

Mala was in bed with Washington.

Noor was at Café Des Artistes.

On the other side of the world, Sophia was having a coffee with Dave at the Landmark.

Chapter 10

South East Asia

"Come on Sophia, tell me everything, about that gorgeous guy we met last night," Dave asked, as he and Sophia had brunch at one of the city's most obnoxious malls. "Where is he from? What does he do? How much does he make? Has he been married? Is he straight?"

"I don't have all that information Dave, but I do know that he moved here a few weeks ago from London."

"Ooooh Sophia, you might not have to leave Hong Kong after all. Did you like the way he spoke? His accent? Did that turn you on? Did you cream your pants? I must say he is gorgeous."

"I know," Sophia said dreamily. "He's such a gentleman. And one can only dream, Dave."

"Dream of what?"

"Dream of being with someone so kind."

"You don't have to dream Sophia, just jump his bones mate! You would *jigi* him right?"

"I definitely would Dave."

"So would I Sophia." Dave winked at her. "Just bang the endearing bloke… or I will." Dave was laughing into his latte.

"I don't want to get attached. I'm leaving Asia, and I don't need any more links, or connections, or distractions."

"Don't be a prude, Sophia, just call him, and make a new friend. Live a little!"

"He wants to take me out for dinner next week."

"Hoorah! Grandma-ma finally found a man to take home. Where is he taking you?" Dave asked.

"I told him I was busy," Sophia sighed.

"Sophia! Why! Why did you tell him you were busy? You really are a dick!"

"Oi!" Sophia was annoyed.

"You shouldn't have told him you were busy. He could be your impetus for sex, drugs and rock 'n roll and ultimately staying here with *moi*."

"No Dave, it's not going to work. I am definitely leaving, and tomorrow I am going to tell Gary. And I'm not going to flake out telling Alister either."

They finished their meal, and Dave felt sad. He really didn't want Sophia to leave. He knew that Craig came at the right time; Sophia had to be less wishy washy and focus.

Sophia got home at six thirty in the evening. Max and Josie were meowing for their dinner. She picked up Max and snuggled him under her chin. Max acted more like a dog. He snuggled up closer to Sophia and rested his head on her shoulder. Josie was meowing incessantly by her feet. She picked up Josie, both cats cradled in each arm. As she walked into the kitchen and served them up a tin of Whiskas each, her thoughts were on Craig.

Alister wasn't home. He was hardly ever home these days, as he was either at Tanya's or at band practice. She had to arrange a time to tell him she was leaving for London, just not today, she thought. She walked into the living room, sat on Uncle Peter's old Victorian armchair and watched BBC World.

Chapter 11

London

Eight weeks had gone by and Mala was reaching another birthday in two weeks. She felt sad and couldn't understand why everyone around her was so happy that she was growing into real maturity. Sharon was planning a surprise party, which she naturally told Mala about. There was still no sign of Noor.

"You have to act surprised, okay *auntyji*?" Sharon was flicking through a magazine.

"Thanks for telling me!" Mala didn't know whether to laugh or cry.

Sharon was giggling out loud. "I have no one else to tell, so I thought I might as well just tell you." Sharon was so matter of fact sometimes. She looked out the window and Noor came to her mind. "I wonder if she's okay."

"She's fine, I think… I tried to call her yesterday but her phone has been disconnected. Maybe we should go down to Paris for my birthday and surprise her."

"Can't leave mum," Sharon said abruptly.

"I wonder how Jeremy is, and how he is taking her swift and unknown departure," Mala asked.

"I saw him last week. He looks terrible, he is a twat and he was with another woman," Sharon said scornfully.

"How long did you want him to wait Sharon? He can't keep waiting around for her." Mala sounded exasperated. "And who knows if she even said goodbye to him?" Mala knew Noor hadn't made any contact with Jeremy before she left, but she didn't want to open that can of worms with Sharon, lest she spit out copious words for lecturing purposes.

"You see, Mala, there is a side to everyone we don't know." Sharon gazed into Mala's eyes. "The only people you should ever reveal yourself to are your family, because they are the only ones who will ever truly forgive you."

Mala felt a stinging pain in her stomach. "I'm confused," she said putting both palms on her belly.

"All I'm saying…" Sharon said, "*Is sometimes the man dies.*"

Both women were in stitches of laughter.

"We haven't been down to Bazica in ages Mala. We should go this week for sure."

"Yes definitely, but it won't be the same without Noor." Mala's stomach ached again. What was this pain, and who was thinking about her?

"Old habits are hard to break precious, but sometimes we have to face changes, which in turn brings new challenges." Sharon was still flipping through a magazine.

"So what is your story Sharon? Why are you so resilient and unmoved by life's challenges?" Mala asked, still with her palms on her belly. She felt like she needed to poo! "Do you ever get affected by anything?"

"My parent's divorce, but that was a lifetime ago. Look how old we are now. And there is no need to dwell on the past. It's so boring to go back there. You can automatically say to yourself… been there, done that, and bloody not going back there again." She was beginning to get into lecture mode.

"Do you think you will ever get married Sharon? Do you want to have children?"

"With all the trauma I see every day, with my kids, the thought of having kids scares me sometimes. Do you want to have kids Mala?" Sharon asked with sincere concern.

Mala didn't have to think twice, she said with a burst of enthusiasm. "No, I am too old. Remember the reader I was telling you about, Krystyna? She said that I had seven children in my last life."

"With who Mala? Let me guess for one hard minute… ummm. Washington?"

"YES!" Mala replied with so much glee.

"Oh my God! You are so predictable… you make me laugh." Sharon was laughing so hard. "From this day on we will christen you *Aunty Pushpa.*"

Both women were once again in stitches of laughter.

Mala's bag started to vibrate and she rummaged into her purse to see who was messaging her.

Sharon was still wiping the tears of laughter from her eyes while imagining Mala pushing out seven children in a wicked village in Africa with Washington, in her last life. Sharon was so glad she was a visual learner. She had a stellar imagination, which always brought humour into her life.

Mala finally dug her phone out of her bag. It was such a mess. All the time. She looked at the message and it read:

"Boo! Guess Who!"

It was her sister. The last time she saw her was almost a year ago. She checked the phone again and realised that her little sister was, in fact, in London. Sharon looked at her friend and knew that it was a family matter.

"Who is it *bungy*?"

"It's my sister, Mila," Mala was still staring at her phone.

Sharon put her hand on Mala's shoulder and said, "Don't sweat the small stuff Mala. Be a good older sister and communicate with her. Maybe this is the time in her life she needs you the most… you both get on so well, and you shouldn't let anyone or anything take that away from you."

"Should I call her back right now?" Mala asked.

"Of course you should. Why are you behaving like a child? She is your sister for God's sake."

Mila was just as gorgeous as her older sister. So beautiful. An Indian Goddess. Petite in her frame, and the face of a Roman angel. She never really contacted Mala unless it was an emergency, and her unexpected visit to London from Manchester was indeed a surprise. Mala hated surprises. Nonetheless, she always tried to accommodate her sister when necessary. Mala wondered how long she was going to stay this time. A sense of unity settled inside her and she was excited to get in touch with her sister and catch up with a member of her family. They began to text each other.

Mala: Hey Mila, how are you. Is everything okay?

Mila: Hi Mala, I'm okay. How are you? I'm at Victoria Station now. Is it okay if I stay with you and Washington for a few days?

Mala: Of course... there is no need to ask. Where are you now? Have you eaten?

Mila: Thank you for letting me stay. I really appreciate it. I am starving. Shall we go eat?

Mala: Let me cook a nice meal for us at home. We can open a bottle of wine and have a chat. Is everything okay?

Mila: Yes everything is fine... I will talk to you when I see you.

Mala: Okay see you in an hour... I can't wait to see you.

Mila: Me too...

When Mila got to the flat both sisters hugged tightly. It had been a while and both of them had aged.

"I'm so sorry Mala, I haven't visited in ages. There has been so much going on in my life. And I didn't know who to turn to... sometimes I think you are the only one who has a brain in our family..."

Mala interrupted. She was already beginning to feel stress and her sister had been in her home for just a matter of minutes. "What's wrong? I hope it's nothing serious…"

They talked and talked for hours, and when they had come to the close of their conversation, nothing new had been revealed. She was again the hamster on a wheel, desperately trying to get off the beaten road for the millionth time. Mala sighed so many times during the conversation that she felt like she was on a rewind button. The book *The Journey Home* came to mind, and she felt like she was reliving the same movie once again. She talked about Maneck, her husband with whom she had borne four children. He was once again in rehab for cocaine addiction. Mala said nothing.

Mala knew there was more. It couldn't have only been about Maneck, because she knew that Mala was not interested in that part of her sister's life anymore. She hardly saw her three nieces and nephew in Manchester and this was not a pity party kind of visit. Mila had something important to say.

Mala decided to make a Chinese vegetable stir-fry and rice. There was nothing else in the fridge except beef, pork and dried black beans. She contemplated making steak but remembered that her sister never ate beef, even though she was so westernized. Mila never touched it because it was against Hindu religion. Mala chuckled at her sister and she heard her mother's voice in her head:

"Bloody young vuns these days, doing naughty tings, playing around vith drug dealers, smoking, going vith black people and not eating beef… such hypocrisy yar… Hare bapare. Vot to do vith this young generation."

After dinner, while Mila was in the shower, Mala's mind drifted to their childhood. She wanted to cry. She remembered protecting Mila when she was ten. Mala was sixteen. That was the last time she saw their mother.

After dinner and chatting about more miscellaneous issues, Mala was still unclear about her sister's visit to London. She hated feeling misinformed. It was two thirty in the morning by the time they went to bed and Washington still wasn't home. As she settled Mila into the guest room, she made herself a cup of tea and sat up in bed thinking about legends, and myths: the Goddess Durga, the Goddess of light and *Shiva*, the lord of creation and destruction. She remembered a story she wrote when she was seventeen:

She shone like the sun as dusk gave way for the moon to rear its creative sphere. Her name was Durga. An alluring Indian woman with an immaculate sense of style and grace. She married a southern Indian man who was four shades darker than her. Her mother was of Persian descent and her milky olive skin glimmered with beauty. Her husband was a merchant and came from a lowly family, but she loved him enough to marry him. Her parents forbade her desires because he was from a different caste and had no money to support his bride. As a young bride, she gave her husband everything.

She cooked, cleaned, listened and nurtured him. She tended to his manly needs and obeyed his instructions. Santosh was happy with his bride. He was the master of his kingdom and she was indeed his slave. Santosh pacified Durga by reinforcing to her that she was the embodiment of all Hindu women. She was everything for which any man could have asked. Without a voice, Durga obeyed. Even when they moved from India to a distant land, both husband and wife remained strong in their bond, until one day Durga learnt how to speak. Her voice was as pure and as soft as an angel; she needed this for her children. She wanted to teach them the real way, not the old ways. Her first baby was a blessing and Santosh was proud. She was a beautiful baby girl, who always smiled and had a healthy appetite for life.

One day Santosh came home after voyaging another land and saw that Durga's belly was swollen again. Another offspring was on the way. This time it had to be male. Santosh was tired; he knew all his hard work would be in vain if he couldn't conceive a son. Another girl arrived and Durga protected her with the strength of Kali. One night Santosh became enraged, casting blame for his miserable plight. His temper flew and a fire soared inside his heart. There was no love, only a distant memory of what used to be. He threw his family out of the house and Durga became Kali, *the warrior Goddess brought to earth to fight the demons. Her daughters were all she had. She was living a waking nightmare with Santosh. Her rage became even stronger and like a tigress she leapt onto Santosh's shoulders. He became* Satan *and his eyes widened as he slowly beat* Kali *to the ground. The light went out and Durga was no more.*

Chapter 12

South East Asia

Sophia came home from a lovely night out with Craig. Alister was sitting on the sofa with Max and Josie. Feeling weightlessly happy and strong, she sat down and told Alister she was leaving. He was happy for her, and knew that he had to work harder to support himself. She comforted him with her plans to leave some money aside for him, just in case he needed to use it. Everything went as planned. She felt another weight off her shoulders.

She went into her bedroom and felt so content. Everything was working the way she wanted and visualised. Dave was wrong about her. She did know what she wanted and she was going to pursue and move forward with all her plans. The only person now left to tell was Craig, even though she felt no obligation to share her news with him. She sat at the edge of her bed, smiling and pondering as she took her shoes off. She fancied the pants off him, but she knew she had to do what was best for her. She had a girlish thought... like a teenage girl... 'if he loves me, he will follow me to London.' She giggled at herself as she switched off the light and fell asleep with the wisdom of peace sustained in her soul, and a very girlish feeling in her heart.

Craig got back to his flat in Happy Valley, threw his keys on the counter, switched on CNN and placed himself languidly on the sofa. He folded his arms behind his head and placed his feet up on the coffee table. He was content in his own space.

He knew he was going to be in Asia for a long time. He was falling for the girl of his dreams. Sophia, he thought, was the kind of woman he had been looking for all his life, and he was going to do everything in his power to hold on to her.

Still, he couldn't quite figure her out. She spoke of Gary, Alister and Dave, but never revealed too much about herself. He liked that for the time being and was going to keep doing things to make her happy.

His mobile phone rang. It was Jennifer calling from London. He pushed the 'silence' button and went to bed.

Sophia walked with a bounce in her step when she arrived at work. It was Monday and she had the energy of a lion. At the meeting, Gary looked angry and the other members of her pathetic team, in need of a serious shift, looked dreary. She, on the other hand, had a strong grip on reality and for once in her life felt focused. At the end of the meeting when Gary asked if anyone had any other business, Sophia put her perfectly red manicured hand up and announced that she was leaving at the end of this year. Silence hung in the air. Gary's molecules and atoms in his body rose to his head again and he looked like an overgrown beef tomato.

As Gary adjourned the meeting, he stopped Sophia and asked, "So, what's the verdict Sophia? We can't wait any longer."

She looked at him, wondering if he had some mental problem, or if he had some mechanism that rejected anything he didn't want to hear. Sophia looked at him and retorted, "Do you have ears, Gary? Did you not hear what I said in the meeting, approximately sixty eight seconds ago?" She inquired as she looked at her watch. "I. Am. Leaving. What part of that don't you understand?"

Gary was bewildered. He had nothing to say, and he was never at a loss for words. But today, he had nothing to say. Absolutely nothing. He fixed his tie and uncomfortably grunted. "Umm… ummm… alright then… alright… ummm…"

Sophia interrupted harshly. "Good, I'm glad we have an understanding now. I will be handing in my resignation on November fifteenth. And I will be getting myself ready for my journey back to London. If you have any problems Gary, we can discuss this matter over lunch, tea, coffee or dinner. Nevertheless, I think I have made myself quite clear. So, there is no room for options or change."

Gary was astonished. His Asian spark plug had turned out to be an *Asian nuclear missile.*

"Gary, I will be at my desk if you need me." Sophia walked confidently back to her office, shut the door, sat upright at her desk and called Dave.

"Hello my darling *Dior* baby doll," Sophia said with a tune in her voice. She felt she wasn't playing the rules of someone else's game anymore.

"Sophia? Is that you? Why do you sound like that? So different like you're on cloud nine? …Did you get laid? Come on, tell me all the details."

Sophia interrupted, with a light hearted giggle. "Nope Dave, I didn't get laid. But I did tell Alister I was leaving. And I told that twit Gary as well."

Dave's heart sank. "You are really going through with it aren't you?"

"Yup. I'm finally following through, David Graham. For the first time in my life, I'm going to do what Sophia Martin wants to do."

Dave was sullen. "That's great Sophia. I'm so happy for you."

"Lighten up Dave. It's time…" She giggled again. "Why the glum voice, you're going to miss *grandma-ma* so much right? Everything happens for a reason, right Dave?"

"I have taught you well my petal," Dave said, with a weak smile. He was going to miss her so much. "Meet me at the IFC tonight for a coffee."

"Sure no problem. See you later my beam of sunshine." Sophia was iridescent as she spoke.

Dave put the phone down and felt lost and empty. He really didn't want Sophia to leave. He was happy for her but not for himself. He had no one in Hong Kong. Sophia was the most honest and sincere person he had ever met in his entire life. Dave was not young anymore. He didn't want to be selfish and he knew Sophia was doing the right thing. It's funny how people get used to each other and suddenly their behavioural patterns become habits. Out of the blue, when people grow wings to fly, we become agitated and feel a sense of unfamiliarity. Dave wondered if he was being completely self-seeking, egotistical and like so many people in Hong Kong, who couldn't live without their friends, cars, mansions and expensive clothes. He didn't want to be like one of them. He made a commitment to himself and Sophia to honour her decision and encourage her to be the best person she could be. Sophia was his best friend and sometimes friends had to leave in order to better to themselves and the people around them.

Craig and Sophia were sitting at Mr. Kim's, a Korean restaurant just off of Lan Kwai Fong. The food was scrumptious, but frankly quite overpriced. Sophia took it upon herself to treat Craig to a romantic dinner, since she had something to tell him. They were holding hands across the table like two lovebirds. Sophia looked radiant. Craig was mesmerised by her and he felt he knew everything about her, her family and her work. He was excited to be with her, and he sensed she was going to reveal something very truthful about her inner self.

He had spoken to Jennifer on the phone in the afternoon because she managed to hunt him down at work. Craig regretted picking up the phone that Monday morning.

"Hello, Craig Matthews."

"Where the bloody hell in Christ's name have you been? For Pete's sake, I've been trying to get a hold of you for the past ten weeks. What are you doing? Why have you been dodging my calls? You've found someone else. Haven't you! It's a chink isn't it… you…"

"Jennifer!" Craig was gritting his teeth as he shouted her name down the phone. "Please stop harassing me. If you called to insult me I don't want to speak to you... now if you speak with grace, we can continue this conversation." Craig sounded calmer. "Is everything alright?" He knew he didn't love Jennifer nor was he in love with her. He cared about her, as was his nature. He would never turn his back on people. He was concerned about her because of their break up. At his age, he couldn't handle the drinking and the antidepressants and her mood swings.

"No! Everything is not bloody alright! When are you coming back?"

"Not for a long while Jenny," Craig said as he shut the door of his office. "I have already discussed this with you. My job is here, in Asia, now."

"It's another woman right? Tell the truth! How dare you leave me in London and go off with all those Oriental girls... I'm... I'm disgusted with you..." Jennifer was crying and shouting down the phone at the same time. She was a mess.

"Jennifer!" Craig was getting agitated again. "Do not speak to me like that. I am at work and need to concentrate. This is why I don't answer your calls, because you act like a spoilt child."

Jennifer cried even more. Her temperament was so hard to handle.

Craig hated it when women cried. "Please don't cry Jenny."

"Don't tell me not to cry. You left me here and I wanted things to be good. I was willing to try... for us. You left me." Jennifer was sobbing on the phone uncontrollably. Poor lady. At her age, she didn't need to be feeling this way.

Craig had to admit that agreeing to take the job in Asia was running away from her and the constant arguments. It was for the best. They were both not getting anywhere and Jennifer knew they couldn't be together anymore.

Jenny was still irate on the phone accusing Craig of having another woman, affairs, sex filed nights and a very murky image of his life. Craig felt sorry for Jennifer and her dark thoughts. He pacified her and reassured her that he would call her later. As he put the phone down Craig didn't want to think about Jennifer anymore.

His only focus right now was Sophia. He snapped back to the moment and tried to dissolve the conversation with Jennifer in his mind. He imagined a telescope and she was very far away, but as he looked at Sophia, her image was large, bright and clear.

As Sophia talked about Dave, Alister, Gary, and even about Max and Josie, Craig knew he adored her. He loved her soothing voice and the way she spoke about her animals in a manner that made them real, alive like an extension of her family. Three hours went by and Craig was still unsure about what she wanted to tell him. He didn't care, at this point, because he felt so in tune with her, as if they were on the same frequency.

After the first silent moment during the whole conversation, Sophia sat back in her chair and spoke.

"Craig, I want to be completely honest with you and in order for me to do that, I might risk the chance of losing something that has come as a blessing in my life. I would rather you hear this from me than from anyone else. And the city is a very small place. Gossip is man's red fire here. What I'm about to tell you... didn't happen suddenly... it's been on my mind for the past four years already."

He was confused. Did she want to marry him? He was utterly lost for a second. Sophia took her hand away from his and took a big gulp of her wine.

"I have made a decision in my life," she said.

"Tell me Sophia. What is it? I'm all ears," he said looking into her dark brown eyes. "I can handle anything. You are the most wonderful person I have met. You came to me at the right time Sophia..."

Sophia leaned back in her seat, adjusted her napkin on her lap and looked deep into his eyes. He had such beautiful eyes – brownish green with flecks of gold. She looked at the table, took a breath and said. "I'm leaving Asia."

Craig was definitely shocked. He looked like a lost puppy. "When?" He asked.

"Before Christmas," she said gazing down at her napkin.

"Why?" He was lost.

"I've had enough of Hong Kong after seven years of it. I think it's time for me to move on. This city we live in has this… propensity to creep up on people after some time. At first it is exciting and carefree, but after a period of time, it isn't fun anymore. People take so long to evolve here. There is not stability for me here anymore. Especially at my age."

Craig sat back in his chair and sighed. He looked at Sophia. She was so eloquent and had such a tight grip on the English language.

"When did you make this decision? And are you certain about leaving? Nothing will change your mind?" Craig was speaking quite fast.

"I made the decision right before I met you. I have to follow my heart. I have to start doing things for myself. I am not getting any younger," Sophia said as she placed her napkin on the table and started to fold the corners of the crisp white material. "I know I should have told you earlier, but I didn't know when the right time was and things have been going so well between us. I needed to tell you sooner than later. I didn't want to walk you up the garden path, for you to find out that there aren't any flowers in the garden."

Craig managed a weak smile. He liked her metaphors and her long-winded soft spoken explanations.

"The last thing I want to do is hurt anyone Craig. Especially you," she said as she leaned forward again.

Craig leaned forward as well and said. "Maybe I'll come with you."

Sophia was laughing. "I wouldn't want you to jeopardise your life for me. That would be silly," she said grinning like a school girl. Craig made her feel so young.

"Where are you going?"

"London," she said still smiling like the Cheshire cat.

Dave sat back heavily in his seat, sighed; looked at the table behind him and felt a stinging pain in his heart. He was perplexed.

Chapter 13

London

Mala was hysterical, she couldn't control her tears. They kept falling and falling like an enraged waterfall, like in Iguazu, where the Mission was filmed. Her tears were relentless, cascading all over her face. She tried to sit down and it didn't work. She tried standing up to control her breathing, but that still didn't work. She was convulsing and all she could do was wrap herself into a little ball and cry into the carpet.

She tried to get up and make a piece of toast. She had lost six pounds in four days. The answering machine read four new messages. She clicked the button and half listened while starring like a zombie at the phone.

The first message was from Noor. "Hey Mala, it's me, Noor. How are you aunty? I haven't been able to get a hold of you for the past four days. I was actually in London for Nikki's wedding but I am leaving today. I'm doing well. Hope you are well. I have some juicy gossip for you and Sharon. I met a guy in Paris, his name is Ahmed and he…" The answering machine released an obnoxious beep and cut her off.

The second message was from Sharon. "Hi Mala, I'm worried about you. Please call me back precious. Washington is so worried about you too. He says he hasn't seen you awake in a few days. Please call me. Better yet, I will come over and see you tonight."

The third message was from Mila: "Hi sis, thanks so much for letting me stay. I had a great time. You are an amazing sister. Thanks for being patient and listening. You are one of the strongest people I know. You are my family and I love you."

Mala began to sob uncontrollably again. She put her palms on her face and began to weep. She began to talk to herself. 'Yellow light around me, yellow light, green light. Green light through my body. Please God make me strong again.' She was desperately trying to envision colour around her. It wasn't working.

Later that evening, when Sharon arrived, she was shocked. Her friend looked awful. She had aged in the past week and her supple olive skin looked ashy. Sharon embraced her friend with trepidation and let her friend wail like a little girl in her arms. After a few mucus filled sobs, Sharon peeled her frail friend off of her shoulder and comforted her.

"It's alright darling. Come on now, it can't be that bad. Let's talk about it. Have you eaten?" Mala shook her head, as Sharon wiped her friend's tears with the back of her palm.

"I'm going to order some Chinese takeout and then we are going to talk like mature adults. This crying has got to cease."

Mala still looked bewildered as her friend spoke. She had no idea where to begin.

Sharon ordered Chinese food fit for a mini banquet of eight. She then sat down and spoke to Mala.

"You know, Washington is worried about you. So am I…and I'm sure Mila is too. What happened when she was here?" Sharon inquired.

"She doesn't know how I feel and how much I have been crying…" Mala started again.

"Don't cry precious! Calm down and tell me everything slowly. Right from the beginning okay?" Sharon was in teacher mode and pacifying her friend at great lengths.

"It's my family... it's my mother..." Mala's lips started to quiver again.

Sharon breathed for Mala as she was speaking to her. "Now, take a deep breath and tell me slowly," she said as she rubbed her friend's shoulders.

Mala's father was a bright man. He was strong, protective and mighty. She adored him and wanted to marry someone like him when she grew up. Like most little girls she was fascinated by her father.

"*Hey Beti vot are you doing in my suitcase?*" He would say in his thick, strong burly Indian accent.

"I'm going with you Papa. I don't want to stay here," she said. She must have been about six years old.

Santosh smiled lovingly at his daughter. "*Go and tell Mama I need my grey suit for trawelling tomorrow.*"

Mala bounced off the bed and went into the kitchen. Her mother, Durga, was making *dhal-puri* for dinner. She was perfect. Her pink sari had splatters of lentil and oil on it. Not visible, but enough that Mala could see.

"*Malsy* (Mala's pet name when she was little), *Vot are you doing here in the kitchen Beti. I thought you vere helping Papa pack?*" her mother inquired as she threw the puri dough into boiling oil. The flat bread puffed up and the golden brown texture gave way to the smell of heavenly bread. With flour all over her hands, she bent down and placed a delicate kiss on top of her daughter's head.

"I was helping him Mama. But he asked me to come and tell you he needs his grey suit." Mala looked up at her mother. Her beautiful skin was so clean and pristine.

"*Hah... hah...*" She said as she shook her head from side to side. "*I vill prepare for him.*" Durga obeyed Santosh like a good Hindu woman. Santosh would leave on business trips every two months and the older Mala got, the more frequent his trips became.

One year later, Durga was pregnant again. The Amani family, all four of them, moved to San Francisco for the arrival of Mila's birth.

On the flight from Bombay to the United States, Mala picked Durga's brain about 'the new ball in her stomach.' "Do you think it's a boy or a girl Mama?"

"*I don't know Beti. As long as it's healthy.*" Her mother said rubbing her swollen belly.

"Do you think it will look like me Mama?" Mala asked with an illumination in her eye. Mala looked exactly like her father. Durga knew that her eldest daughter had the spirit of a tigress. Like the queen of the jungle, whose name would shine in bright lights one day. Durga was smiling at her daughter. She was so bright and so inquisitive. She was rummaging in her cookie monster backpack for her favourite book, *Animal Daddies and My Daddy*. She picked up the book and began to read out loud, before falling into a deep 8 hour sleep.

In San Francisco, life was not easier for Durga. She had to get a part time job as a real estate agent, tend to the house and take care of her daughters. The latter was never a chore, but she wished Santosh would help. But he never did. It was his practice to always command which sometimes turned into barks.

As her daughters got older, the more open minded they became, especially living in a foreign country. But through this metamorphosis they were indeed teaching their mother to be more vocal and stand up for her rights. Women had rights in America after all.

Mala recalled one day when she walked into the house with too much makeup on her face. Her mother was not impressed at her sixteen year old's attitude or mask of war paint on her face.

"*Mala Amani, your father is going to beat you if he sees all that rubbish on your face. Hurry up and vash it off,*" she said looking a bit frightened.

"Ma stop being so Indian and start being universal please," Mala said in such a cocky manner.

Durga knew exactly what her offspring was talking about and took pride in her daughter's liberal attitude. She had a strong inclination that her daughter would definitely go far in life.

"*And vhere is that sister of yours? Huh? Huh?*"

"She's at the mall. She said she'll be back before dinner and before the tyrant gets home." Mala was looking for something to eat in the fridge.

"*Is that what you both call him?*" Durga seemed stunned.

"Yeah dude... he's a tyrant. What happened to him? I used to respect him, but now I've lost sight of all his intentions and actions. He grosses me out. Sometimes we get so angry we want to punch him..." Mala banged the fridge shut.

"*Hush Mala! How can you speak about your Papa like that?*" She had her fingers up to her lips.

"Easy Mom... it's called freedom of speech. You should try it sometimes. It might help to keep the peace in this house. Don't be so naïve, we can hear him yelling at you almost every night. He's scary and psycho. Nobody's father acts like him. It's unreal." Mala looked at her mother as she spoke.

Durga was quiet. Her daughter went over to her fragile mother, lifted her chin and sunk her eyes deep into her mother's; she burrowed her soul into her eyes like a melding of energy.

"Has he ever hurt you Ma? Like physically? Because if he has, you know we can report him to the cops. Abuse is a big no-no in this country." Mala was very serious in her tone.

Durga pulled her chin out of Mala's grip and pushed her hand away. "*Ve are Indian Mala. And it is nobody's business vot goes on in our household.*" She didn't want to talk about it anymore, lest Santosh walk through the door and see them conspiring. He always commented about how Durga failed at bringing up his daughters with dignity and respect.

At dinner, the girls sat in silence while Santosh ranted and raged about business matters and how he couldn't afford so many things. "*I vish I had a son,*" was his regular request to the universe. But there was never any reply or reaction from the powers above him.

An argument emerged that night. One that played over and over in Mala's life. At her age, she couldn't handle the stress of this particular memory anymore. She snapped back to the dinner table sitting next to her sixteen year old self. On reflection, she wondered, if she wasn't so vocal that night, if her destiny would have been different.

"What is so great about having a son? We are much better don't you think Mila?" Mala asked very boldly at the table.

Durga was playing with her food as she moved the okra, lentils and peas all over her plate, like a child.

Mala noticed her mother and decided to include her in the conversation. "So, Ma, what do you think? Aren't we better than sons…?"

Santosh interrupted Mala, as he slammed his spoon down harshly onto the plate. He leaned forward and as he spoke, and particles of food were spraying out of his mouth. "*I think you hawe no respect and you hawe no right to speak like that at the dinner table! You hawe a big attitude problem. Stop! And I mean it. Stop! Acting Amrikaaaan! Do you understand? Do you understand?*" he asked again, pointing his spoon in her direction.

Mala looked down at her plate. He was so scary when he was in a rage. And was this all because of money? They weren't joking when they told her that money was the root of all evil… what a skewed world she lived in.

"I'm not acting American, Papa I am just being sensible and telling you that the old ways don't work anymore and…" Mala was almost pleading.

'*ENOUGH! Mala Amani! You are a bhayband Sindhi and you vill obey your father.*" He screamed as he threw his utensils in her direction. Mila was sinking lower and lower into her seat.

"I don't have to listen to this. It's so boring and restricting. I can't grow up like this," Mala said as she stood up and placed her dinner plate in the kitchen. Her father was still hurling abuse at her.

"Can I please go too Mama," Mila asked as she slowly got up from her seat. Mila didn't want to stay at the dinner table and followed Mala into the den to watch the tail end of the *Cosby Show*.

It was after dinner that life changed for the entire Amani family.

Both sisters heard screaming which they thought was a bit more intense than any other days. There was crashing glass and crying which added to the recipe of 'a stupid marriage.' As they ran out of the den, they saw Durga lying on the floor with blood seeping out of her head. She was laying semi unconscious on the floor. Santosh had gone too far this time.

"Oh! My God! What did you do! Are you crazy?" Mala was whining at the top of her lungs. She sounded like an injured hyena. She was also trying to protect her sister at the same time. She tried to get close to her mother to see if she was alive, or breathing, or something. The man she thought was her father was foaming at the mouth. He was extremely unstable.

"GET OUT OF MY HOUSE! BOTH OF YOU, AND NEVER COME BACK. I DON'T VANT TO SEE ANY OF YOU EWER AGAIN IN MY LIFE!"

The girls ran out of the house and Mila was shaking like a leaf; they had nowhere to go. Mala made it to a pay phone and called her best friend Joyce. Mala and her sister spent three days there. When they reluctantly came back to their house, Durga wasn't there.

Twenty four years later, Durga had risen… or was it Kali…

Mala handed Sharon the envelope Mila brought with her to London. Inside was a letter and a newspaper clipping. Sharon took a deep breath and read slowly. As the pieces of the puzzle started to materialize, Sharon realised why her friend was in such dire straits. And why her emotional wellbeing and her paradigm had been shaken, stirred and served to her on the rocks.

Noor was not impressed with her friends; she thought they were uncaring and selfish for not calling her back. She had a great time at Nikki's wedding. All she could think about was her so called 'best *aunties*' and how they were behaving in such an intolerable manner. She was going to call Mala and Sharon and give them a piece of her mind. She didn't know what to say, yet, but she was going to tell both of them that they were the worst friends she had ever met in her life. She sulked the whole night at Café Des Artistes. She didn't for a second grasp how egocentric she was being. Nevertheless, she still sent a very cutting email.

Just wanted to let you know that we are having our grand opening of Café Des Artistes next week. It's over a period of five days. Many important people from around Europe, mostly my father's friends of course. I will inform you what day is appropriate for you to visit Paris.

Her email was scathing, condescending and holier than thou. She clicked on to Cainer.com to check her horoscope. It read:

Sometimes change is like a debt collector. It catches up with us no matter how hard we try to hide. Sometimes, it is more like a marauding beast. As long as we keep out of its way, it will rampage right past us. How can we ever tell then, what shape change is likely to take next? The answer, of course, is we cannot. But it doesn't matter. As long as we do our best to avoid it, it will either catch up with us or it won't. Are we are now standing on the street yelling. Change come and get me? There is no need to put out such an invitation. It knows where you live and it's on its way.'

She had absolutely no idea what it meant.

Chapter 14

South East Asia

Craig hadn't called Sophia in two days and she was getting worried. She wanted to kick herself for telling him that she was leaving. She was sitting on the sofa at home hugging Max when the phone rang. She jumped like a teenager praying it would be Craig.

It was Dave. Sophia sounded a bit annoyed. Dave was harassing her about the details of why Craig hadn't called her. He convinced her that it was because he felt rejected.

Sophia sounded forlorn. "I don't want to talk about this now Dave…"

"Run away Sophia. Run away… and no, we don't have to talk about this now, but as your friend I think that it would be wise for you to get it off your chest. Release, girlfriend." Dave was smiling. Sophia was not.

"Why do you pretend to know what is best for me Dave Graham? Why do you constantly give me the shiftiest advice anyone could receive? And why do my issues thrill you? Do I look like a script for a soap opera? Why don't you take a moment to look in the mirror and work on yourself for a change? Do I feel gutted? Yes, I do. Do I wish I met Craig earlier? Yes, maybe I do… Do I wish that maybe I should stay in Asia? Yes, possibly, I do. Do I need to go to London? Perhaps not, but I would like to think that I am not a wishy-washy type of person and hope that whatever decisions I make, I can be firm and strong in my thinking and perhaps come out a winner. Do I feel old and cross? Yes. I. Do. Are you happy now? I realise that there are worst things going on in the world right now, like what we see on the news every day. Nonetheless, I am still human and I have needs and desires, and I need to find myself. I am losing myself here and if that means I lose the most enchanting man I have ever met in my life, then so be it!"

Dave was dumbfounded. "I'm… I'm so sorry Sophia… I never meant to make you feel like that."

"You didn't. I don't want to speak about Craig anymore right now… and I would like some respect please. When I am ready to discuss the intricate details of my life and my psyche with you, I will indeed give you a call."

"Take it easy," Dave said with a tinge of sadness in his voice.

"I will. Don't worry your pretty little fashion designer head. Now, if you have finished, I would like to hang up like a dignified woman without having to hang up on you. Goodbye. I will speak to you tomorrow." Sophia hung up the phone without waiting for a reaction.

She was puzzled and restless. She wished she could rewind time and make Craig come into her life earlier. She was so stubborn. Why couldn't she just stay in Asia? What was the big deal? She was her own enemy and was desperately trying to prove the idea of stability to herself. She needed to need just herself – not Alister, not Craig, not London, not her cats and not Dave. Just herself.

Craig didn't know what to say to Sophia. He didn't know how to approach her anymore. He felt childish and like a grief stricken boy. Love makes people do funny things when it's not looked upon in its purest form. He was in a daze and didn't want to speak to anybody. He had to get a grip of himself and realise that timing is everything. Sometimes in this life time we miss the train that has everything we want on it, everything for the taking. Sometimes we miss that train and just sit back and wait for the next train to come along and hope the same things emerge. Or sometimes we desperately chase the passing – hoping and praying with all our might that we can catch up. Questions percolated in Craig's mind. He had to snap out of this feeling and start doing things that made sense to him only.

The phone rang. He jumped. Answered. It was Jennifer. Again.

Chapter 15

London

Sharon finished reading the contents of the letter and let out a sigh. "Listen precious, it's all in the past and things are better now. Remember that the present is what we should be focusing on. I know it's hard, but you are smarter than that and I know you can pull yourself together."

Mala wasn't sobbing anymore, she had no more tears to cry. Her eyes were still wet and her face was dragging, drab and grey.

Sharon continued, "You are a strong woman Mala. I don't need to tell you that right?" she said as she pushed the hair off Mala's face and pulled it behind her ears. "Come on, it's your birthday soon. You can't look like this. You'll scare everyone way."

Mala smiled at her friend underneath her panda eyes. "I don't want a surprise party Sharon. I don't want to do anything at all actually."

"Oh come on, don't be such a *bungy*. It's only once a year. And none of us are getting any younger. It will be a good celebration. And I'll arrange something small. Maybe just you, me and Washington. Nobody else." Sharon was thinking of all the phone calls she needed to make to cancel Mala's party.

Her birthday was next week and she didn't want to make a big deal about her age. She wanted the day to go by like any other day, but she knew Sharon and Washington were not going to let that happen.

"Do you think I'm a strange oldish lady?" Mala asked, as she looked at her sagging skin in the mirror.

"You are an angel Mala, you have accomplished so much in your life. Don't fret over the past, now you know the truth. So embrace it. Things happen to us for a reason. Nothing in this life is a coincidence. Maybe this letter had to come to you before your birthday, so you could start over again, with a new perspective on life. There is no need to be sad anymore. You have emerged from the darkness and the light will guide you."

Mala adored Sharon and knew they would be friends for the rest of their lives. "Thank you so much Sharon for being so patient with me."

"No worries precious. That's what I'm here for. Now, we are going to talk about something else, not because I don't care, but because I need you to pull yourself together and look at this day as a rebirth. I brought you something."

Sharon pulled out her wallet and took out a 'Miracle Card.' Every card had a number and a message. Usually it was a spiritual message carrying an abundance of inspiration. She handed the card to Mala.

"Now, this is for you. Every time you feel sad and this letter from your mother pops up into your head, just take out this card and read it."

Mala took the card and she saw it was the 44th card in the deck. 44. She wondered what the significance of these numbers were. She was going to find out. The card read:

"The essence of energy is love and energy is everywhere."

"Thanks Sharon, that's beautiful. Are you sure you want to give this to me? I don't want your deck of cards to be incomplete," Mala said as she put the card to her heart chakra.

"Don't vorry aunty, it's meant for you." Sharon was shaking her head from side to side.

"What does 44 mean?" Mala asked.

"I don't bloody know. Do I look like the local oracle to you? To me, it's just two numbers that look exactly the same, like *tvins!*" Sharon replied in her Irish-Indian accent.

Mala was smiling some more. "You are really special *aunty* and such a wonderful friend. Thank you for being in my life."

"Always here for you Mala." Sharon felt relief. "Oh yeah, have you heard from Noor?"

"Yeah, she left a long message about her cousin's wedding and some guy called Ahmed... she said she called you," Mala said as she was moving away from her past thoughts.

"OH. NO! Here we go again... but to be honest, I never heard from her. I have also been so busy at school lately, I didn't have the time... I just feel so busy."

"Is everything alright Sharon?" Mala asked.

"Nothing I can't handle love. One of my boys has been diagnosed with severe ADHD. He's like a Long Island iced tea gone wrong. He has the violent side of the disability too. I think he's just frustrated. Poor boy," Sharon said as she pulled up her sweater and revealed a purplely, pinky, yellow bite mark on her forearm. It was huge!

"My God, that is so massive Sharon. Why did he do that?" Mala asked as she stared at the injury on her friend's arm.

"Yeah my little Korean boy, Jun Do. He did this to me. The one who's been coming to the centre for years. And now they say he's too violent for the other children, so they want him out. I told Noddy Neil to inform his parents right away, or the board of education will shut us down. Do you know what he did instead?" Sharon said as she was getting a little upset.

"What... what did he say?" Mala inquired.

"Noddy Neil says in a whisper, mind you, so that I am the only one who can hear him carefully, '*Asian kind are very sensitive about their children and we don't want to ruin her weekend, so we will keep the matter on the back burner until it happens again.*' I was so mad.

What if he hurt one of the other children? Then whose weekend would be ruined hah? So I've been in countless meetings with the boy's psychiatrist, this week, so we can prescribe him with another cocktail of drugs. Poor boy."

Sharon and Mala continued talking about other aspects of their lives until they were both giggling. Actually, until Sharon forced Mala to giggle. When Sharon accomplished what she set out to do, she felt it was time to leave. She left her friend's flat that night, knowing that she was going to be alright.

Mala felt so much better. Her friend was a miracle in human form. She was an amazing character. Her mother was right, people do come into our lives and manifest themselves as angels to give us hope. Mala decided to have a hot bath with lavender oil and a touch of bergamot, to make sure all her troubles would be washed down the drain. A bath always helped her release tension. And while all the pain was going down the drain and into the pipes and washing away into a river of blue, she smiled at the thought of knowing that she still had her most precious sister anyone could have asked for. Mila was a light and a spark. An amazing light. Mala knew that she had to make a commitment to look after the only family she had left.

After her long soak in the tub, Mala made herself a cup of hot chocolate and crawled into bed. She opened the envelope and decided to read the contents of it for the last time in her life, before ripping it up into insignificant pieces and flushing them down the toilet.

The newspaper clipping read:

Asian Man Hangs Himself after Leaving Suicide Note

An Asian man known as Santosh Amani hung himself in his San Francisco home last night. Police found a suicide note next to his body revealing that the reason he didn't want "to be on earth, is because he failed as a father and husband." His family are scattered around the world and investigators say they are looking into locating members of his family. Mr. Amani's lawyers say his daughters are living in England.

The dramatic undertone of suicide amongst Asian men has caused a stir in the media. Researchers in India are asking the question, is there too much pressure on Asian men to be the sole bread winner of the Family? More on Page 8.

Santosh had become a statistic. Mila didn't seem affected by the article, because she was actually happy he was dead and she hated him with a passion. Mala was going to teach her sister to let go.

She next unfolded the letter and began to read:

Dear Mala and Mila,

You are probably wondering what happened to me and how come I have suddenly come back into your life. After I heard about what happened to your father, I immediately located one of you so I could let you know what was going on.

The night I left your father was a tragic day and I realised I shouldn't have left both of you with a man like him, but I had no choice. I was a prisoner in my own home, and I couldn't take it anymore. Since the day your father and I got married, he has behaved in an abusive manner towards me.

I never wanted to leave both of you and I can't begin to tell you how much I missed you. Not one day goes by that I don't think about you. I know your father told you I was dead. I told him to say that because I didn't want you girls to ever become like me or follow in the same footsteps as me. I spoke to your father once a year to ask how you girls were doing and he told me of your whereabouts. Mala, he said you hadn't spoken to him in over twenty years. You disappeared after college and he never heard from you again. He was heartbroken and so was I. I knew Mila was in Manchester and believe me, so many times I wanted to visit, but I just didn't have the heart. I want you to remember me in a positive light and know that sometimes things in this lifetime don't always work out the way they should. As your mother, I bless you every day and pray all your dreams come true.

I realise it must be a shock to suddenly hear from me, but you must know, my disappearance was for both of you. Your father would not have paid for your education if I was still around. I did it for you both. I wanted you to be smart and know that no matter what anyone takes away from you, they can't take away your spirit or your education.

My address is on the bottom of this letter, if you want to contact me. I understand if you don't. Please forgive me.

I adore you my angels.

In Love and Light,

Mama

As she put the letter down to breathe, Mala knew one thing was certain: her mother's English was definitely better. She had no more emotion to give. She ripped the letter and newspaper clipping into very delicate pieces and gracefully threw them all into the toilet.

Noor finally got a hold of Sharon. She was on bulldozer mode, ready to give her little Irish friend a piece of her mind. Sharon was so excited to hear her voice.

"Oh my God *aunty*! Where have you been? So much has happened since you left. I don't know where to begin…"

Noor interrupted. "So much has happened to me as well. And no one bothered to even contact me when I left messages for both you and Mala…" Noor sounded testy on the phone and rather cutting.

"We had a lot of crises and…"

Noor interrupted again… "Oh I suppose your crises are so important that you can't even pick up the phone to call a friend after I have left so many messages."

"I know Noor, but we haven't heard from you in two months and there is a lot going on right now…" Sharon was still smiling as she spoke.

"I have to be completely honest with you, Sharon. I need to get this off my chest. I am really quite troubled by the fact that you and Mala didn't even bother about me."

Sharon was quiet and stunned. Her smile vanished quickly off her face and she went into lecture mode.

"Well… let me tell you something Annabelle. Life does not revolve around you and there has been a lot going on in other people's lives. Not just yours. Have you tried to call Mala? Do you know what kind of state she has been in the last week with her family? You don't even know do you? So please do not think that you are high and mighty and we have to run every time you decide you want us in your lives."

"Mala is fine," Noor snapped. "I spoke to her on the phone five minutes ago. She said everything is great, so I have no idea what you are talking about."

"I see," Sharon said.

"What do you mean?" Noor asked sarcastically.

"Maybe she didn't want to tell you Annabelle because you haven't been around. And… you're the one always doing the talking. Do you ever listen to anyone but your own misguided voice?" Sharon said fiercely.

Noor was taken aback. "I know I am terrible at keeping in touch and I did try to contact you and Mala but no one ever tells me what is really going on in their lives…"

Sharon interrupted almost growling. "Annabelle. I am really busy and I don't have time to get into the details of your royal life right now. I have so many things to do."

"How insulting Sharon…"

Noor tried to continue but Sharon butted in like a bullfighter. "Which part, the fact that you keep running away or you have no grip on reality or the part where you don't understand the meaning of friendship, or that obnoxious email you sent us about the opening of your *daddy's* restaurant or the fact that it is always up to you to decide when it is convenient to be amongst friends or family?"

Noor was silent. In a whisper she said, "I don't know what you are talking about." Or maybe some phlegm was stuck in her throat. She sounded hoarse like she was itching to say something, but it was stuck in her like a ball of festering regret.

"Then this conversation is over."

"Fine!" Noor's voice suddenly had some projection.

"You constantly behave like a brat. Why don't you grow up a little Annabelle? It's getting very boring you know… the dull details of your flighty life."

Noor snapped. "I did not call you to get insulted Sharon Connell."

"For Christ's sake, Annabelle, stop behaving like that. It's disgusting!" Sharon was shouting.

"Don't you dare talk to me like that! Who do you think you are Sharon? And at our age, how dare you have the nerve to shout at me."

"Key words, Annabelle, *supposed* to be; maybe you need to find out what the meaning of friendship is before you start stamping your feet. And let me remind you that, for some of us, in life, we create our joys and sorrows long before we experience them. And you, my dear friend, are making an issue out of nothing. When you are ready to come down to earth and show your true self, then give us a call. Oh… and another thing, if you really care about Mala and I as friends, you won't harass her and pick up the phone to try and find out what happened. Just trust me when I tell you she has been through something very major in her life. And, frankly, she doesn't need someone like you bombarding her with your gossip or details of your diva life. In case you've forgotten, it is her birthday tomorrow. Don't forget to at least wish her a happy one. Now that I have said my piece, I have to go. Bye!"

Sharon hung up the receiver and her blood was boiling. Noor was an egomaniac and had so much growing up to do.

Noor was on the other end listening to an ear deafening click. She was mortified and extremely angry. She thought for one second about calling Mala to find out what was happening in her life, but as fast as the thought came in, it quickly vanished in seconds, like a whisper lost in the trees. She sat in her father's house, once again, all alone. She had everything, yet she had no substance. She felt like she had become a bowl of jelly on the inside and she didn't know what to do.

The next evening, La Bella Luna had a kicking vibe. Washington, unfortunately, couldn't have the time off for Mala's birthday, so Sharon decided Mala's party would have to take place at Washington's workplace. Sharon was late, of course, and informed Mala that she had a surprise for her.

Mala sat in a booth and waited for Washington to finish his set. She reflected on how strong she felt today. Memories of her childhood seemed to fade into an abyss and all she wanted to focus on was now – her life with Washington, her bond with Sharon and her deep love for Mila. She wondered why her sister didn't call.

Sharon then arrived with Mila. Mala's smile reached both corners of her face. She was just manifesting the love she had for the three people who now sat with her on her birthday. She was content. Sharon placed a brown paper bag on the table, which looked like it would have some alcohol in it, but she instead pulled out three tiaras.

"What is this Sharon?" Mala asked.

"It's a bloody Tiara. What does it look like *bungy*?" She placed one on each of them and then began her speech.

"This is a tiara of strength. Every time we get together, we have to wear these and this will give us '*aunty pover.*' Now, since it's your birthday I would like you to put yours on first and then we will follow."

Mala slowly placed the fake tiara atop her head and thus gave the royal go ahead for Sharon and Mila to follow. The three ladies sat at La Bella Luna the whole night – drinking, laughing, eating and strengthening their union with each other, as Washington and his band painted the atmosphere with sweet, soulful music.

Four forty five in the morning, it was time to go. As Washington, Mala and Mila walked into their flat in Hammersmith, still with tiaras on top of their heads, Mala felt like a queen and a new woman. This birthday was small but truly significant. She would keep this night in her heart forever. She thanked the universe for one more day of life and drifted gratefully to sleep.

Chapter 16

South East Asia

Three and a half weeks went by and Sophia was sitting in her flat with boxes of her 'stuff' ready to be shipped. She had four more days in Asia. Her leaving party at *Bloomberg*'s was fun. Although Gary actually looked sad, she thought, for the first time in his life he didn't look like a twit.

"We are really going to miss you Sophia. I hope you leave with good memories of this place. I want you to know… if you ever come back to Asia you will always have a place here," he said with a very sincere look on his face.

"Thanks Gary, that's very kind of you," Sophia said with golden candour.

The party was in the office and a huge banner above her desk said, 'Good Luck Sophia.' She was so happy to go.

After her last day of work, packing and having a daily coffee with Dave at various spots became her normal routine. It all seemed to be happening so fast. Still no sign of Craig, she felt she was slowly getting over him and placed him amongst other men she dated. She was going to call him the day before she left, out of courtesy, to say goodbye. Alister was happy for his sister and was looking forward to having the flat all to himself. He was feeling more grown up.

Sophia eventually finished packing and shippers were slowly moving her boxes out of the house. This was it, there was no turning back and she felt good. No more wishy washy ideas. She felt stable. She couldn't wait to arrive in London for her new beginning. She was happy her father was excited to see her and he was coming to pick her up in his Jeep.

Daniel Martin never remarried and he lived a very simple life. He worked as a carpenter after his divorce and lived quietly in a house he bought for himself and his kids in Surrey. As his children got older, he kept the house in top shape because he wanted either his son or daughter to take care of it when he passed away. His ex-wife, Margaret, never saw the house and he had lost contact with her after her brother Peter died. Daniel couldn't wait to see his daughter and spend Christmas with her. He didn't know what to buy her yet.

Although Sophia felt guilty that her brother was going to be spending Christmas alone, without her, she bought her father a new tool kit and put it in her suitcase, because she didn't want to rummage through the boxes when she arrived. She wasn't sure if she was going to live in the same house as her father or if she was going to mortgage a flat on her own. For the time being, she had already told her father she would be staying with him for a while.

The only thing Sophia had to do now was to party like a rock star before she left. She was going to do that with the love of her life, Dave.

They were sitting at Starbucks on Staunton Street one evening discussing Sophia's departure.

"I'm going to miss you loads Sophia," Dave said.

"Me too Dave, I wish I could take you with me."

"I promise I will come and visit."

"You better. We have to keep in touch. I've heard that after people leave Hong Kong, they lose touch because they don't want to be reminded of the loss."

"Don't worry sunshine, I will definitely keep in touch. I promise I won't cry at the airport, I'll just cry *after* the airport." Dave continued.

"Oh Dave," Sophia said with a melting sensation in her heart.

"So, are we going to have a party before you leave?" How do you want to say *au revoir* to Asia darling?" Dave asked with a very small tinge of happiness in his voice. It was faint but still clear. "And by the way, has Craig contacted you?"

"Nope," Sophia answered with confidence. "I will call him to say goodbye."

"You will?" Dave was shocked. "Why? For what reason?"

"For my piece of mind Dave. Maybe he's dead, who knows?" Sophia said casually.

"Don't be so dramatic." He wasn't impressed with that casual attitude.

"Me. Dramatic? Come on Dave. Who is the least dramatic person you know?" Sophia was laughing.

"You! Oh boring one," Dave said in his most camp voice.

"You don't think I should call him, do you?"

"What for? Leave him behind, where he belongs. Instinct always gives you a signal, or… it could be gastric flu. It's going around. And tell me… what are you going to say to him?" Dave asked sarcastically.

"I'm going to say, 'Hey Craig. It's Ultra Woman. Just wanted to say goodbye to an insensitive coward like yourself and hope I never see you again, because if I bump into you, I will probably walk away. I hope you have a good life. I needed some closure so I can leave you behind where you belong.'"

"Are you really going to say that?"

"Nope!" Sophia said smiling.

"You really are such a wimp! Smooth talker."

"Oi!" Sophia snapped in her British accent.

"Honestly Sophia, we need to have a leaving-do for you. And you need to say goodbye to the city before you live the life of a *grandma-ma*."

"Dave I want you to know… you are the loveliest person I have ever met in my life, and in the seven years I've been in Asia, you have been my pillar of strength, and without you in my life… it's so hard to think about you not being a part of my life. I adore you Dave and

I care about you immensely. Thanks for being an amazing friend. And for looking after me in Hong Kong while I was on this journey." Sophia was tearing up as she spoke. She knew her time in the city was definitely over.

"God Sophia, it's times like these I wish I was straight." Dave was smiling at her.

They got up to leave and as they walked out the door a Chinese boy with dyed blonde hair, brown teeth, gold chains and tatty tennis shoes holding a camera snapped a picture.

"Wait." Dave was calling the boy back; he was about to run. The Chinese paparazzi always pretended they were in a gangster movie and would frequently draw attention to their target from their obnoxious actions, such as running away for no reason. The small Chinese boy looked at Dave in confusion.

"Come back," Dave yelled after him.

The boy was hesitant, as he didn't know if Dave was going to punch him or not.

"Now, here is another one. Hold on. When I say go… you take the picture." Dave was making silly hand gestures as he spoke.

The paparazzi boy was smiling. Dave had made his night. His teeth looked like they were encrusted with mud. He knew this next picture was going to fetch him far more money than the previous one.

"Alright, here we go. One. Two. Thr…" Before Dave could say 'three,' he planted a kiss right on Sophia's mouth. Suddenly, there seemed to be an ocean of lights flashing, while voices in the background were saying "wahhhhhhhhhhh."

Friday rolled around and Sophia, once again, looked stunning. Dave wanted to dress her in *Christian Dior*, especially after all the gossip that splashed all across the Chinese tabloids after – 'the kiss.'

Sophia felt like she was getting married. She was standing in Dave's office on Friday afternoon, trying on a plethora of different garments, from couture to casual.

"Wow sunshine. You look delicious in that. One day couture will be out on the streets like you'd never believe. It's art. Try on the other outfit." Dave was looking at Sophia like a Goddess as he spoke.

"I would never go out in this Dave! No more fancy catwalk attire, I want to try on those silk hot pants," Sophia said as she pointed to the clothes on a rack behind Dave's desk.

"You, in hot pants, are you serious? You would never go out in those. Would you?" Dave asked as he handed her the hanger with the ensemble already intact.

Sophia came out of the dressing room in Dave's office and strutted around in a pair of emerald green hot pants and a cream sleeveless polo neck sweater.

"WOW!" Dave exclaimed.

"What? What is it Dave, tell me the truth, does my bum look big in this? I know you can see some skin. You're absolutely right, I would never go out in this," she said as she tried to turn her head to look into the mirror.

"Wow, you look so amazing petal. Like a sex kitten. *Me. Ow. You're hot girlfriend you're gonna set my office on fire girl.*" Dave was speaking in a Southern Tennessee accent. He should have been a radio theatre actor. His voice was amazing. He could imitate anyone.

"I'm definitely not going out like this. Nope. No way," Sophia said as she began checking herself out in the mirror. She actually looked like a very mature model.

"Why not *grandma-ma*? You have to leave Asia in style. Be a little bit adventurous in your life."

"Nope! I'll try on the other outfit." Sophia walked back into the dressing room, which was equipped with full length mirrors all around, an armchair, a small side table, a dressing table with a variety of *Christian Dior* makeup and a small ensuite. It was a princess's dressing room.

"Sophia, you looked gorgeous in this green outfit. Why won't you wear it? I'm so upset," Dave said, pouting like a puffer fish.

"I won't leave Hong Kong with SLUUUUT attached to my name Dave."

"Why not? It will be fun! I can see the headlines now: *Slut girl is actually a closet prude and Dave Graham, once again, has transformed a woman from her basic self, into a sex God!*" Dave was pretending to read the headlines in the air as he motioned his hand across the atmosphere.

Sophia came out of the dressing room and she looked superb. Dave was sizing her up. She was wearing a backless, fire engine red, chiffon dress with a scoop neck. Dave was busy hemming it up to, a little above, the knee.

"This is the dress Dave," Sophia said as she twirled around like a ballerina.

"I know petal, this is really the one for you." He had pins in his mouth as he was hemming up the dress some more.

"Now, all we need to do, is go into the stock room and have a rummage. It'll be so much fun. Come on, quickly, let's go!" Dave had finished with the alterations and was dragging Sophia down the hall to the magical room of 'accessories.' Sophia had been into the stock room before and always felt like a kid in a candy store. Dave got a basket and was doing some 'internal' shopping. Sophia was giggling like a school girl. Dave put all the items on his 'shopping list' for which he was billed at the end of the month with an 80 percent discount on everything. In the stock cupboard Sophia and Dave proceeded to act like two girls playing dress up in their mum's closet. After five hours of pretending to be oversized Barbie dolls with a magnitude of clothes and accessories, trying on eighteen outfits and sixty eight pairs of shoes, Sophia was exhausted. So they went back to Dave's office and ordered a bottle of champagne.

"I had so much fun today Dave. Thank you," she said as she sipped on her champagne.

"Me too darling. But it's not over yet, the next step is to now parade our gorgeous selves around Hong Kong tonight."

"I can't wait. I'm so excited." Sophia was pouring another glass of champagne for herself.

"Go on, get going sunshine, I have some real work to do before we meet tonight. I'll see you later."

Sophia stood up, walked to the door, with four *Christian Dior* bags in hand and said. "You rock David Graham. I'll see you later. Me. Ow."

Dave was almost falling off his chair, he loved it when Sophia unleashed her 'beast'.

"*Au revoir*, sunbeam. I'll see you at 9:30 p.m." Dave said as he escorted his elegant friend out of his office.

As the two friends parted, both thought how much they were going to miss each other.

Sophia got back to her flat and walked into her empty room. The only piece of furniture left was her bed. She hung her dress on the door to ensure wrinkles wouldn't appear and sat on the edge of the bed. She was going to call Craig, but decided to hold off on the idea till she was ready to board her flight. Alister wasn't home. Max and Josie were already on their way to England. She jumped into the shower and began her pampering and preening session, before her last wild night in Hong Kong.

At 8 p.m., Dave was still in his office dealing with another *Tai Tai*, whose obnoxious daughter was graduating in three days and needed a dress for her ceremony being held at the Regent Hotel. Parents of private schools had so much money to waste, he thought.

He was going to have to get dressed at the office again. He knew dealing with Mrs. Chan and her daughter was never easy.

His ensemble was a purple collared shirt with Edwardian cuffed sleeves, a pair of black and silver pin stripped trousers, and a pair of dark blue shoes. He managed to find an aqua blue pair of sunglasses, which would be placed perfectly above his head. He had a system of how to put his sunglasses on without messing up his hair. He wanted Mrs. Chan and her daughter to hurry up and get out of his office.

Chapter 17

London

Sharon was with Mui Mui in West Hampstead. They were painting. Sharon wasn't feeling good today; she was still livid about Noor's outrageous behaviour. She wanted to tell Mala, but didn't want to sound like a child. She started to imagine herself let go of the situation but it wasn't working. She was sullen today.

After the painting class, she drove Mui Mui home and picked up her mother from Shepherd's Bush. To get her mind off Noor and the meaning of friendship, she turned the stereo on as 'Beautiful Day' by U2 blared out of her BMW speakers. Sharon felt like she was releasing tension as she sang along.

Once she reached Shepherd's Bush, she picked up Sandy. "Hey mum, how are you today?"

"I'm fine darling." She looked at her daughter. "You look sad doll, what's wrong?"

Sharon always counted on her mother to know her best.

"I'm not happy with Annabelle mum. She thinks she is high and mighty and I really despise people like that, but it's hard when one of your best friends acts like the royal family, when it is so undeserving."

"Have you told her how you feel pet?"

"I hung up on her."

"Sharon, my darling that's not very nice or appropriate." Sandy sounded a bit disappointed in her daughter. At her daughter's ripe age, she should know better.

"I know… I know mum, but I am so tired of her pretending that life is going to end all the time."

"Don't worry precious, you do what makes you happy, pet. But I do have to comment on one thing…" She paused as she cleared her throat. "Try and hold your tongue. Sometimes you sound like your father."

Sharon was silent. Maybe her mother was right, she should learn how to hold her tongue… sometimes. They drove the rest of the way to St. John's Wood, in silence. When they got home Sharon called Mala.

"*Aunty*, please meet me at Bazica in half an hour."

"Sure no problem. I can only stay for about twenty minutes. I'm on my way to a yoga class. Is everything alright?" Mala was frantically packing her yoga gear as she spoke. She really didn't want to be late for her lesson.

"I'm feeling rather disillusioned by the concept of friendship at the moment. Please meet me soon," Sharon said as she got ready to leave the house.

At Bazica, Sharon told Mala about her conversation with Noor, how she hung up on her and how she felt bad about reacting so harshly.

"Maybe she needed someone to tell her. I mean, I agree with some of the points you brought up to her… well, to be honest, I agree with a lot of what you said to her. I haven't heard from her in ages either. She sent me that silly email as well and she didn't call for my birthday. At the end of the day, I've got so much going on in my own head, I let her silliness slide. I don't want to dwell on it, I don't want bad karma." Mala was very sincere when she spoke.

"So, you totally agree that she was behaving like a child again, right?" Sharon asked, as she puffed away on her smelly cigarette. The laws for smoking indoors needed an adjustment.

"Yeah, I do Sharon, but we are in a friendship not a marriage. Friends come and go, but family lasts forever," Mala said with wisdom and strength in her voice. "You know what Sharon, life is too short to be dwelling on things we cannot change. If we keep creating issues just for the hell of it, then we will never grow. I am surprised at you Sharon, these kinds of things have never affected you before."

"I know, that's why I feel so strange. My mother implied that my tongue should be held. She made it seem like whenever I speak my mind, I sound like my father."

"Do you feel like you act like him?" Mala asked.

"Well, I am my father's daughter, love."

"Well then, maybe you do... and there is nothing wrong with that. Is there? Come to yoga with me. I think you will have fun," Mala said like a true *aunty*.

"Nah, I'm going to go home and sit with mum," she said in a sullen voice.

After Bazica, Mala walked around the corner to her yoga class at High Street Kensington. She loved the class and her yoga master, Kamal. Today, he was teaching his students about balance. He also gave her insightful messages about the meaning of each *chakra* in one's body. Each major point in the body represented a colour. Yoga began to give her an in-depth view of ailments and blockages caused by imbalance. Before her birthday she had so many blocked *chakras*, and only now at her seasoned age, was she beginning to release. Her mission towards healing was underway.

During her yoga class, Mala meditated on Sharon and Noor; she sincerely missed having them both around at the same time, especially at Bazica today. She was going to let them deal with their friendship issues, while she dealt with the meaning of her existence and her purpose in this life. Slowly and through time, Mala was indeed becoming more spiritually aware.

While Mala was sitting in the lotus position – imagining a cylinder of white light travelling through the crown of her head, Sophia and Dave were at the Kee Club.

Chapter 18

South East Asia

"Sophia, I have to tell you that you look mind blowing tonight."

"Thanks Dave."

"May I do the honours of showing you off, Sophia, as my *Christian Dior* creation?"

"Nope. Absolutely not."

"Why not!" Dave asked with semi agitation. Sophia looked like a movie star.

"Because I want to remain a mystery," Sophia said with a deep lustre in her eyes.

"A mystery or a bore darling? There is a very fine line between the two, you know." Dave was sipping more champagne.

"Dave can I ask you something? I would like to ask you a huge favour… will you call Alister occasionally to see how he's getting on?" Sophia looked worried again.

"Sure thing petal. Don't worry. You know he'll be fine right? I will definitely look in on him. Now wipe all those track lines off your face. We are going to have to invest in millions of dollars of plastic surgery if you keep frowning like that."

Sophia's train of thought was interrupted by an obnoxious, drunk lady at the bar. She caught Dave's eye as well. She was completely incoherent and was bellowing like a bull, as if chastising a matador, as she yelled down her mobile phone.

"Look Sophia, check that thing out." Dave's mouth was curled up in absolute distaste. Her demeanour was so uncouth.

"She is an embarrassment to women."

"Sounds like it could be her boyfriend, let's listen."

"Don't be so nosy Dave," Sophia said as she tried very hard to look away, but the scene was like a movie.

"Why not, it will be fun." Dave looked mischievous.

The two best friends were suddenly jolted out of their conversation as they watched the outlandish and very peculiar lady scream in her drunken stupor, down the phone.

"You said you would be here! I'm not yelling! I feel so stupid sitting here... I'm here on my own! I'm not pissed... I'm not drunk! ...No. I'm not! ...Don't tell me what I am... What?... What did you call me?... That is the rudest comment ever! ...Whatever... I am embarrassing you?... How?... Oh, I see, you are Mr. Big Shot... Who. Do. You. Know. Here! ...I don't see anyone you could possibly know here... Everyone here that I'm looking at, is not your type! ...I told you where I was! ...I'm at this Kee Club place!"

Sophia was laughing. "I don't want to watch anymore. She is behaving like a wench. The bouncers should escort her out."

"I've never seen her before." Dave was looking at her up and down. Who was this bizarre woman?

"Maybe she's a white *Tai Tai*," Sophia said turning back to her glass of champagne.

"*Tai Tais* don't talk like that in public my petal." Dave said with both his eyebrows so far up his forehead he looked like the Joker.

"*Tai Tais* are human too."

"Sub-human. But nevertheless, they would never go AWOL like that in public, especially at a place like this."

"There is always a first time for everything Dave Graham."

Sophia and Dave indulged in salmon pate, oysters, escargots, filet mignon, lobster and crème brulée. They also polished off two bottles of champagne and one bottle of red wine.

They reminisced about their seven years together, and it was customary for Dave to make fun of Sophia. They exuded unity and at midnight decided to leave the club and as Dave put it, "mingle with the commoners."

They decided to head up the street to check out the scene. The two lanes in Lan Kwai Fong were packed. They stayed for ten minutes and in that short space of time, Dave wished he had suggested they go somewhere else. He didn't want to make an issue out of the spectacle he just witnessed, so he whisked Sophia away to the Captain's Bar at the Mandarin Oriental Hotel. That was indeed more up their alley.

There was something he noticed but did not want to bring to Sophia's attention. He saw Craig, not alone, but with that crazy white *Tai Tai* who was yelling down the phone like a rabid dog at Kee Club.

Craig was unshaven – which is why Sophia probably didn't recognise him. And the lady he was with was persistent with her berating of him. More than once, she almost fell flat on her undignified face. Dave thought Craig looked like a bum.

At the Mandarin, Sophia was having fun. He wanted to tell her about the marvel he spotted an hour ago. But that was in the past and he didn't want to ruin the moment. Instead, he made sure his best friend remained the most graceful, dignified, elegant woman in all of Hong Kong. Craig was history and so was that absurd episode he was glad not to be a part of.

Craig did notice Dave and Sophia walking away. All he could do was gawk. She looked amazing! He wanted to ship Jennifer back to London on the next flight and run to Sophia. He wanted to kick his old self for letting her go. And he wanted to strike himself even harder for not being consciously robust. He was beginning to harbour severe animosity for Jennifer, which wasn't his initial intention. However, her visit was totally unexpected and thus gave Craig a reason to be completely horrible to her. Especially after he noticed the woman of his dreams float away into an abyss of the city.

He grabbed Jennifer by the arm and dragged her down D'Aguilar Street towards Pedder Street. He couldn't wait to shove her in a taxi and get home.

"You are the most embarrassing woman I have ever met in my life. You are disgraceful. You have no etiquette. You act like a prostitute. You are rude, arrogant and plain stupid. You said you came here to get me back? You failed Jennifer Ball. I never ever want to see you again."

Jennifer was sobbing again; and still, between tears was trying to be the winner. "You bastard! You left me and promised me you were going to marry me. You told me things were going to be good and…"

"Stop blubbering!"

"Piss OFF Craig!" She screamed.

"No! You piss off! You are leaving my house tomorrow. I don't care if you sleep on the street. You have no idea how much you have distanced yourself from me." Craig was fuming like a dragon.

He hailed a taxi and shoved Jennifer into the backseat. He wasn't rough with her, just firm.

"Happy Valley please," Craig said trying to be polite.

Jennifer had her hands in her face and was crying again like a five year old. She was in such turmoil. Craig was silent and immobile, as hard sedimentary rock. He was expressionless. Like *Amah Rock*. He didn't even want to look at her. She had arrived ten days ago and since her arrival into the city, Craig had lost himself. He couldn't wait for her to leave.

When she arrived, Craig wasn't happy or sad. He never wanted to end up hating her. He had always wanted them to be friends. He wasn't a bitter bloke. He wasn't going to become affected because of one bad relationship experience. He missed Sophia intensely and felt stupid for not contacting her sooner. The only thing on his mind was to get Jennifer out of his life, and Sophia back in it again. Jennifer had to go.

She stopped crying and was staring out of the window. She loved Craig and knew she had blown any chance she had of ever being with him again.

When they got back to Craig's flat, Jennifer began packing. The last thing he said to her was, "Have a good life Jennifer and know that we are no more. This is the end. Please make sure you have left by the time I'm back from work tomorrow."

Jennifer packed in silence as tears streamed down her face. She knew she lost the finest relationship any woman could have ever asked for. She pushed him to the edge one too many times, until he fell off and flew away.

Chapter 19

London

Mala laid in bed with Washington on Saturday morning. She was feeling vibrant and connected to the world. Yesterday was the first night in months Washington was off work. They didn't go out. It was getting colder so they decided to buy a real Douglas Fir tree and decorate it together.

While Christmas carols were playing in the background, Mala and Washington made sweet love. He was always gentle and his soft chocolate brown skin against hers made her soul feel warm. When he touched her, a wave of passion would fill her spirit. When he kissed her, it was like a chocolate rain of ecstasy pulsating through every inch of her body. For three hours they were connected to each other through love, touch, insight and sound. She could feel her red *chakra* open and bloom like a flower. The ripples of uninhibited love gently jolted through her body as she slept. In the morning she was glowing and her light brown cheeks were shining like ripe tomatoes.

"Good morning baby," Mala said as she turned over to kiss Washington. He embraced her, pulling her closer to his body. "Don't ever leave me okay Washington."

"Why would I do that? Don't think like that. You are my diamond."

Mala snuggled up closer to Washington. She adored this man. She knew attachment was bad and only led to pain, but she didn't care. She wanted Washington with her forever. They were totally in sync; spiritually, mentally and physically. She couldn't imagine being in love with anyone except him.

After a hearty breakfast, the couple took the tube to Camden so Washington could buy the army boots he wanted. Washington had to get ready for work later that evening and when he left, Mala felt strangely abandoned. It was an awful feeling. She knew it was the physical and material aspect of herself longing to feel his love.

Instead of sulking, she turned on her stereo. Kamal had encouraged his students to buy a CD called *A Hundred Thousand Angels*, which he recommended for home use.

She began to imagine herself encircled by a golden light as the music commenced. She could feel herself flying through a mystical rainbow of colour. As her red *chakra* began to slightly close, she felt a sense of peace. She wanted to stay in this realm forever. Mala slowly descended back to earth as she heard the last part of a message Noor was leaving on her answering machine.

… "I am coming back to London for a few weeks. I really want to see you and Sharon. I need to call her. I have a project I am doing and need both of you for research and…" The answering machine cut her off again. She was being so long winded. Again.

Mala smiled. She was happy for Noor, she felt like one of her *aunties* was on a mission for rebirth and growth. It would be wonderful to share her thoughts with Noor. She couldn't wait to see her.

Chapter 20

South East Asia

Sophia was at Kai Tak airport with Dave.

Alister had already said goodbye to her at the flat. When he said goodbye to her, he was playfully pushing his sister out the door.

"I'll visit soon," Alister said.

The elevator door shut and Sophia felt happy. He was jubilant. Exactly what she wanted to see.

On the way to the airport and for the first time in seven years both friends had nothing to say to each other. Sophia's heart sank.

At the check-in counter Dave started talking. "When will you be back petal?"

"Soon. But not too soon."

"I don't know what Hong Kong is going to be like without you."

"Don't start Dave. I'm not dying."

"I know, but a part of me is," Dave said with a very heavy sigh.

"Oh God Dave! That is so dramatic. Please stop, you are going to turn this farewell into something soppy, wet and unflattering."

"Should I sing for you instead?" he asked with a half-smile.

"Nope!"

"Come on, don't deny me before you leave. That's just vicious."

"Me? Vicious?" Sophia said playfully punching Dave on the arm. "Alright then, go ahead and sing then."

Dave had a sensational voice. He was a great performer. He began to sing: "*Ain't no sunshine when she's gone mmmmmmmmmmm mmmmmmmm. Ooooooooooo. Ooooooo mmmmmmmmmm...*"

"Dave stop!" People were looking at them. The strict old lady behind the counter who was doing the check in looked at Dave sternly from behind her reading glasses. Dave looked back at her and started singing louder. "*Doo do doo do do do mmmmm.*"

"Dave, I'm begging you to stop." Sophia was in stitches of laughter. She could always count on Dave to make a grand entrance or departure.

"Did you call Craig?"

"Oh! Crickey. It completely slipped my mind Dave. Thanks for reminding me. I'll do it before I board the flight."

"No! Don't!" Dave said with urgency. He wanted to kick himself for reminding her.

"Why not?"

"Just don't."

"Why?"

"Please don't."

"Why not Dave? It's no skin off your nose if I call him."

Dave looked worried. He didn't know how to respond. "I umm... umm... a... um... I saw him with someone else," Dave said hurriedly.

"Riiiiiiight. Is this another one of your jokes Dave? ...where did you see him?" Sophia chuckled.

"Last night." Dave looked away.

"With whom?"

"The crazy white *Tai Tai.*"

"You are outrageous!" Sophia was laughing hysterically.

Dave was stammering. "It's true…"

"Okay Dave. I believe you."

"So, don't call him. Okay."

"Okay."

"Swear Sophia. Please don't call him."

Dave didn't want to push the issue any further; he didn't want her to lose that smile. Or argue with her. At the gate, Dave squeezed his best friend tightly. "Miss you already sunshine."

"I'll call you as soon as I get to London," Sophia said as she squeezed her friend.

As they parted, they knew they would be seeing each other very soon.

Dave walked back to the train and a tear fell from his eye.

Inside the terminal, Sophia located a pay phone. She had to return all her electronics back to *Bloomberg*, so she was not contactable until she reached her father's house. She dialled Craig's number. She had summoned it up by heart.

"Hello?"

"Hello…" It was a lady's voice on the other end. Sophia was a bit confused.

"Um… I think I have the wrong number." Sophia said, recalling that she didn't make mistakes with numbers or sequences of numbers.

"Whom are you looking for?" asked the voice on the other end.

"I'm Sophia Martin… I'm looking for Craig Matthews."

"I'm afraid he is still at work. Is it urgent?"

"No… nothing urgent. Whom am I speaking to?" Sophia was upset.

"Jennifer…would you like to leave a message?"

"No... no thank you... have a nice day." Sophia hung up the phone and recognized that voice.

She didn't know whether to be angry at herself for not listening to her best friend; angry at Craig for being dishonest and ignoble; angry at Dave for not pointing out Craig and the white *Tai Tai* Jennifer to her on Friday night.

She couldn't wait to get on the flight and leave this God-forsaken continent.

Chapter 21

London

Sharon was really sick. She had bronchitis and was in bed for three days. It was getting cold in London and the weather didn't agree with her at all. Every time she coughed it sounded like she was going to bust a lung.

"Sharon why don't you go and see the doctor?" Do you need anything? Can I make some soup and bring it over?" Mala asked with genuine concern.

"Nah love, I'll be fine. Went with mum to buy a heater yesterday. It's so bloody cold outside! The heater doesn't seem to be keeping me warm. I have three duvets on."

"Oh my love. Please let me know if I can bring anything over." Mala didn't like having her friend like this. So she decided to change the subject. "Noor is coming in today right?"

"Oh really? She didn't tell me," Sharon said while coughing into the phone.

"Really? Again? She left a message on my phone, telling me she wanted to see both of us because she had a big project going on and she needed us for research."

"I see! So that's what we are to her now. *Ree. Search.* The girl has no idea what she wants in her life." Sharon was rolling her eyes.

"Sharon, don't be so bitter. Maybe this is her way of making up with us. Forgiveness is the key. Don't be such an old *aunty*. Why are you still mad at her?"

"Do you know she sent back all the books she ever borrowed from me? Do you think that's nice?"

"No not at all. At least she is giving them back to you." Mala wanted to be optimistic.

"She sent one of yours too... I can't remember the title right now... it's Mr. Nobody. Mr. Everybody. Mr. Spectacular... I can't remember Mala."

"Mr. Nice?"

"Yes, that's it. What a boring title. No wonder I couldn't bloody remember the bloody book. Who would ever want to read a book with a title like that?" Sharon was coughing again.

"It's actually a very good book. You should read it some time."

"Maybe when I'm feeling better precious. I really feel like crap Mala." The coughing wouldn't cease. It was so difficult for Sharon to make coherent clear sentences without a horrendous sound coming out of her mouth.

"Whoa, Sharon, take it easy. I really think you should go see a doctor."

"I will precious, but not today. I am knackered and freezing. I can't get myself out of bed."

"I'm definitely coming to see you after my yoga class. Maybe you should come with me one day. Yoga helps to clear blockages... like your throat is hurting, right; the throat area is your blue *chakra* – the centre of communication, speech and the effect of the spoken word of truth."

"I see," Sharon replied with absolute scepticism.

"Listen Sharon, it's really interesting. Now, the reason you have a bad cough is because this *chakra* is blocked. And what you need to do is imagine a blue light going through that part of your body because..."

Sharon interrupted, "It's too profound for me. I want to imagine myself on a warm beach with a bunch of hot hunky men giving me a massage. All this yoga malarkey is too much for me to handle."

"Are you going to be well enough to meet Noor, when she calls you?"

"*If* she calls," Sharon said with sarcasm. "You can tell her I can't articulate properly and that I don't want to get out of bed. Tell her I will see her when I'm feeling better and when my blue *chakra* is functioning."

Sharon released another ghastly session of coughing and sputtering. She was wheezing so much on the phone.

"Sharon, that sounds so disgusting. Stop smoking!"

"I know love, I have to."

"Did you smoke today you little Irish chimney?" Mala said with a tinge of annoyance in her voice.

"Yeah I had three."

"What! You are ridiculous! You really sound like a truck driver when you cough like that."

Sharon was laughing and coughing at the same time. Her voice was rough and edgy. "How do you bloody know what a truck driver sounds like?"

"I just do."

"And what does that sound like Mala?"

"Rough. I have to go to yoga now, I'll come by and see you later."

"Okay precious. I'll just be here driving down truck driver's coughing highway."

As soon as Mala put the phone down it rang again. She was irritated because she didn't want to be late. She scowled at the phone.

"Hello?"

"Mala!" It was Noor.

"Hey Noor! I can't wait to see you." Mala's irritation had dissipated and she was smiling like the *Joker* from *Batman*.

"Bazica in 20 minutes?" Noor said with excitement.

"Yes, for sure. I'll be there." Mala gave up contemplating Master Kamal's tutelage today. She was already distracted. She put her down jacket on and got on the tube. She couldn't wait to hear about Noor's escapades.

Noor was already at Queen's Gate Terrace when she called Mala; she just wanted to stop off at a boutique she saw on the opposite side of the road before she met Mala. She didn't want to call Sharon, she was scared.

Fatima was covered from head to toe when Mala arrived. Fatima smiled at Mala and asked. "Should I bring three cappuccinos?"

"No, just two today," Mala said with discomfort which gurgled from the depths of her voice box.

Fatima looked worried. "Where is the little one?"

"She's sick with bronchitis. She smokes too much."

"I know," Fatima said as she looked down on the ground with her dusky trail of peppered silvery grey light, shining from her astounding almond eyes. Her soul always spoke a very ancient language, one of the wisdom embedded in the land from generations of Persian ancestors, who were indeed royalty.

Mala sat inside waiting for Noor. She was late, as usual. Fatima came back to the table with the two coffees while staring at something outside the window. She was squinting her eyes, so they looked even more oval.

"Is that Ms. Noor?" Fatima asked squinting even harder.

"Oh my God!" Mala was stunned. Noor had gained about thirty pounds in the last three months. She was huge. And her arms were popping out like thick Spanish sausages out of her long sleeve sweater. Mala was shocked. How could her friend let herself fall into a pit like that? A pit of despair, hopelessness and a sheer reflection of being weighed down. The unrecognisable – but still vaguely beautiful woman – walked over to Mala.

"Mala Amani *auntyyyyyyy*." She bent down to give Mala an over confident bear hug. The chair moved to the side almost tipping over the drinks. "I have so much to tell you," she said as she sat down in the chair which offered the most space between her and the table.

Mala was staring at her in awe. Fatima's eyes flickered like lost galaxies as she stared at Noor. "It's so good to see you." Mala revealed.

"You look different Ms. Noor," Fatima said as she darted her eyes away from the contrast of her mesmerizing eyes. "It's good to see you. *Inshallah*. Please enjoy your cappuccino," she said as she walked away from the two friends.

"So, did you call Sharon?" Mala asked.

"No, I thought you would, you know, save me the hassle."

"She's sick," Mala said in a stressed tone.

"I see." Noor was unimpressed or uncaring. Mala couldn't quite figure it or her out.

"So what have you been up to?"

"So much. My father's restaurant is coming along. The opening was great. I'm writing a book; I've met the love of my life and I am so happy with my life. I've been waiting for this for so long. You know all those emails from Preston… well… I've decided to make them part of my memoir," Noor rambled on.

"Wow! That is wonderful. I am so happy for you too."

"What have you been up to *auntyji*?" Noor asked with slight lack of interest, dotted with a notion of obligation.

"Well," Mala continued. "I have joined a yoga class and have been writing a journal. So much has been happening with my family…"

Noor interrupted, "Really?" She was not as fizzy with her demeanour as she was when she walked in. "Well. I'm writing an actual book. And we have to discuss if you are really thinking about writing a book too, because I don't want us to have the same things in it."

"That would never happen Noor."

"Why not, you know way too much about my life, you might… steal my ideas…"

"What?" Mala was stunned!

"Yeah, it's called Intellectual Plagiarism."

Mala was laughing. "Okay Noor."

"I'm serious. Mala." Noor was looking savagely into Mala's eyes. She was not joking.

Mala didn't know what to think of this woman sitting in front of her. She had changed so much in such a short space of time. She tried to think of all the good in Noor and change their conversation about Noor's book including all the nonsense about intellectual plagiarism.

"So, tell me about your love life. You just said that you met the love of your life."

"I don't know if I should tell you. In case you put it in your book. I have to protect myself." Noor smirked as she sat back in her white plastic chair, filling it with her whole being.

Mala was astonished and stunned again. No wonder she had put on so much weight. She was protecting herself too much.

Noor took out her tiger printed note pad with matching pen and stared at Mala. "Come on, now start spilling the juice."

Mala's blue *chakra* started to close up and her yellow *chakra* started to twist and turn in knots and she felt a thick lump travel up her mouth. The engine of energy travelling through her was enough to combust a city. Was Noor really the person she knew? Who was this blubbery figment of her imagination who had swallowed her friend and turned her into a lascivious bowl of pudding? She began to write with her mini cocktail sausage fingers.

"Now, Sharon said something about a big drama you had with your family or something, can you tell me more about that?"

Mala felt intense heat around her. She wanted to clout Noor.

She imagined a sea of green light travelling through her body and a golden light encircled around her.

"Well, Noor, I don't really feel like discussing it like this. Maybe at another time when we are more relaxed and talking amongst friends."

"Oh I see, so you want juice about Ahmed, but you won't spill the beans about your life. I see how it works now."

Mala was disgusted, "I have no idea what you are on about."

"It's called theft. Intellectual theft. At least I am being honest and telling you I need you as research."

"What has happened to you Annabelle Noor?"

"Nothing at all, people change, you know."

"Yes, people change and you have changed for the worst. You have no clue about life, friendship and change. You seem to have regressed." Mala was being tortuously honest.

"My father was right about London, it's full of pretentious people. And you, Mala Amani, should watch yourself. You are beginning to sound more and more like Sharon. Stop letting that little Irish monster influence you."

Mala was laughing to herself. Pretentious. Noor was the pinnacle of pretentious. She was the wizard of all the potions and spells associated with pretence, farce and undignified gelatinous absurdity. She was reflecting all of her insecurities on Mala and it was obvious.

"So are you going to tell me what happened with your family? Or have I just wasted my time?" Noor asked as she began to pack up her pathetic miniscule stationary kit.

"I guess I have wasted your time then, because I'm not in the mood to be branded as research today," Mala said scathingly.

"Well, I'm sorry if I wasted your time, I thought we could at least have a decent conversation before I jet off to Paris again. Hopefully, we'll catch up soon." She smiled at Mala, and pretended to leave a business meeting.

"Bye Fatima darling, you look sensational. Hopefully, I'll see you soon." She kissed Fatima on both cheeks; actually, she didn't even make it to her face, they were air kisses floating in an abyss of coffee aroma from distance lands.

"By Benji. It was great to see you again." He was looking at her in awe. He used to think she was stunning. She turned to Mala again and with a very stern look on her face said, "Hopefully, we don't have the same things in our written manuscripts when I become a best seller Mala, because that would be tragic. Tell Sharon I said hi and I will be contacting her for some research shortly." She then waddled out of the café, clicked on her mobile phone and sashayed like an obese duckling to the other side of the road.

Mala was still sitting in Bazica. She felt like she had walked into a play, something historical like *Brittanicuss* by Racine on stage, and had forgotten all her lines. It was the most unusual experience Mala had ever encountered in her life. She couldn't wait to share it with Sharon.

As soon as she got to Sharon's house she spilled the beans about everything.

"That stationary bit is good."

"Yeah matching pen and everything. So *aunty-ish*."

"No Mala, so *child-ish*."

They talked more into the night, and Mala did some yoga poses to ensure she was calm. They talked about how they wanted to see their friend excel and flourish, not be weighed down by Ahmed or food or her father, or whatever else was making her want to protect herself.

Sharon was so tired she was already half asleep on the couch while Mala was recapping the whole episode in her head over and over again. She thought about money and how it assisted in the growth or decline of one's attitude and perspective on life. Sharon and Noor had cash flow – an abundance of it – but they were so different. One let it go and the other cradled it like a disease.

Sophia had been in London for three days already. It was two more weeks until Christmas. She missed Alister and Dave so much. Her father's house was so big and grand and very English, precisely the space she had been craving for. Space and time were so important for her at this maturing stage of her life. Her father had set up her room overlooking the patio into a sensation of life, nature and abundance. The scenery was breathtaking. The countryside was always a very romantic spot for Sophia. She loved the English side of her heritage, ancestry and beauty of noble times of knights and gentlemen, horses and the ecstatic landscape of healing and renewal.

Sophia's father was never home until nine every night. He worked very hard. He owned his own company and he and his team were doing some design and carpentry work for a new restaurant at Heathrow airport. Daniel was a hardworking man.

Sophia was still in her flannel pyjamas and loved the thought that no one else was in the house. All she could see was the many trees outside the house sprinkled with light droplets of snow. It was freezing.

She lit the furnace and called Dave. They spoke for an hour on the phone. His steadfast humour coupled with the atmosphere of Sophia's blanketed life at her father's house made her feel unity, connection and joy.

Dave promised he would be in London for the New Year's celebration. She couldn't wait and was ecstatic about the thought of seeing him. She was feeling quite comfortable in England.

Chapter 22

Paris

Noor decided she and Ahmed were going to London for the New Year's celebration. He was staying in a suite at the Hilton in Paris which was voraciously comfortable, adorningly mesmerizing and quite erotic. The suite looked like a balcony from the set of a movie. Her veranda overlooked a rose garden. It was breathtaking, to say the least.

Ahmed was the son of a very rich oil merchant who also opened up a bank in Egypt. It was quite bizarre, because no one really understood the roots of his wealth. Nevertheless, Ahmed and his older brother were the products of trust funds, laundering, borrowing, selling, buying and loaning to people. The brothers were known as 'The Sharks' in Paris, and always had beautiful women around them. They were the life of all parties and every woman's desire of a 'catch.' They lived a life of absolute pleasure and debauchery. 'The Sharks,' never let up. They knew they couldn't be with a Parisian woman because their father would banish them from the inheritance like dogs. They were traditional under a very fake façade of internationalism and fickle global citizenship. They were characters.

Noor met him for the first time at an art gallery in Venice. Mr. Noor had sent Annabelle to meet these two distinguished rich men. They were not Indian, but they were of Persian descent and they had similar values to their own heritage.

Noor was swept off her feet by Ahmed. He was the total opposite of Jeremy and had the qualities and stance of Fitzgerald's *Gatsby*. He was a rock and roller, and knew how to cradle every situation like his pet. He knew how to stroke, feel, touch and play with situations and people for his own advantage. He had this strange gift, but used it in a very selfish, demeaning way.

They had been seeing each other for a few months and already, he was pampering Noor for his advantage. He wanted something from her, but he wasn't sure what it was yet. He was sniffing the situation out like a curious fox, looking for his prey to play.

In the suite, Ahmed sat in his robe with his feet facing obnoxiously towards the rose garden. Noor was filing her nails and pleading with him to go to London.

"Ahmed, are we going to London?"

"I don't know Annabelle, I might have to go to Italy for a few days."

"On New Year's Ahmed? Really?"

"Yes Annabelle." Ahmed sighed as he took off his bathrobe and switched on the BBC. He was watching Market Watch with his legs sprawled open.

Noor was upset. She was lying on the bed and she felt really fat. She had stretch marks all over her body. She was really getting old.

"Ahmed, please don't leave me alone for the holiday," she pleaded.

"We'll see Annabelle," he said staring into the TV.

"I wanted to introduce you to my friends."

"I thought you said you didn't have any friends in London. Why didn't you tell me? That means you lied to me when you said you didn't have any friends there." Ahmed turned to look at her sharply.

"They used to be my friends." Annabelle was inching her way towards Ahmed.

He turned his back on her again and said, "Please let me watch this on TV. It is really important. And after this I'm going to play tennis with my brother… and then I'm not sure." Ahmed wasn't even talking to her. He was watching Alan Greenspan on TV, talking about the global economic climate.

"Shall I meet you after tennis?" Noor asked like a rabbit.

"No, no Annabelle, please…there is no need to do that. Why don't you go shopping or something? Or go get a massage or go to the gym for a workout. And then call me later."

Noor was so deeply hurt. He was acting so arrogant and rude. He wasn't like that this morning when he was on top of her like a wild jaguar. Now, all he wanted to do was watch TV. And why did he mention the gym – was she getting really fat? She got up and hugged him and he didn't respond to her physical needs.

"Annabelle go get my wallet. Take some money out and go pamper yourself." He was fixed on the TV as he waved his hand towards the direction of the dressing table. "Take however much you want."

After taking his money, Noor got into the shower and didn't know if she was really happy. She gazed sadly in the mirror. She didn't recognize herself. Everything looked like loose, over-used terrain. She looked away, not wanting to look at all the dimples and dents of blame and regret. She almost started to cry, but was interrupted by Ahmed's knocking on the door.

"Hurry up Annabelle. I need to take a shower. I smell of sex and I need to take a crap!"

Somehow his interruption made her feel slightly better. She knew that Ahmed might be the one for her this time.

After his long hot shower, Ahmed made his way to the Country Club with his brother while Noor was desperately trying to find some clothes that fit her. She walked out of the Morgan shop and felt like her heart was actually embedded in her cellulite. She felt intense shame. She stopped by a salon and a Venezuelan beauty named Margarita was standing inside the shop. She looked at Noor up and down and they discussed a cellulite treatment that would help with edema, tension and elasticity. Seeing that Noor was happy about doing the treatment, Margarita escorted her into a beauty room. She put on a full body stocking while a large vacuum cleaner-like machine sucked on her loose skin.

After forty five minutes, Noor didn't feel any thinner; she was sore all over and her dimples looked deeper. She paid for her session and hurried back to the Hilton. When she got back to the room, Ahmed was in a suit, talking with fervour on the phone.

"Yeah *shua shua*… no problem… yeah… yeah… I heard, Kibran told me… man that stock crashed and burned dawg! …yeah… yeah… *si. si.* Don't worry… *va bene… va bene… ciao… ciao.*" Ahmed's mother was from Sicily, a pure contradiction of what his father really wanted him to marry; hence, his Italian accent and grasp of the language.

Noor flopped herself on the bed.

"Hey girl where have you been? Come to papa." Ahmed was a little bit tipsy from the six Bloody Marys at the Club. He inched closer to Noor, but she pushed him away. "What's the matter Annabelle, is this because I won't come to London with you?"

"Yes," Noor replied with a pouty expression. It really didn't suit her at that age.

Ahmed sighed and turned the TV on again. "Okay… okay… we'll go then."

Noor was excited and happy. She could switch on and off like a light bulb which was so unhealthy. "Thank you Ahmed." She kissed him gently on his nose. He pushed her away and sniffed a big snort as he pushed his hair back and sat on the sofa with his legs sprawled wide open in his usual stance.

"Listen Annabelle, I have an important dinner engagement tonight with my brother and my father. He is arriving tonight. Business matters, you know… I'll pick you up after dinner. Don't stay here alone. Just go back to your father's and I'll come and get you later… Okay."

Once more in her life, she knew that she had to *'recreate herself anew in the grandest vision she held of herself...'* That night she waited for him until two a.m. Still no sign of him. She was getting nervous. She took a taxi back to the Hilton and waited in the lobby until six a.m. Still no sign of him. She took a taxi back to her father's house. And once again, cried the whole ride back home.

Chapter 23

London

New Year's Eve. There was a hum and a vibration circling the earth, which felt like angels dancing the tango in pairs.

Most of the world heralded in the new calendar year with an abundance of revelry and celebration. A feeling of release, liberation from the past and warm welcoming for transformation and change was rocking in everybody's spirit.

Mala and Washington were at La Bella Luna with Sharon.

Noor was at the Ritz with Ahmed, his brother Kibran, his father, his mother and his beautiful Sicilian cousin, Fontana.

Sophia and Dave were having dinner at the Sheraton.

And Craig was all by himself, at his flat, in Happy Valley.

In London, at the countdown, everyone was holding up their glasses. Kisses were flying in the air, champagne was flowing, streamers were being popped and people were smiling.

"I think we should start walking around the streets now, see what we can find." Sharon was talking over the noise. She was ready to leave La Bella Luna.

"Let's go then *aunty*."

"What about Washington?" Sharon inquired.

"He has to stay for the rest of the night. I already told him we would see each other later."

They waited for him to finish his set, and Mala kissed him passionately before she left. His divine melody was so mesmerizing. The sounds of energy and clarity always made people feel so happy around him.

"I love you baby. Happy New Year." Washington lifted Mala off her feet. "Be careful out there okay. Call me if you need anything."

As Mala and Sharon inched their way out of La Bella Luna, with ecstatic beats and a wink from Washington to Mala, family and friends were on their phones wishing each other another year of goodness.

Mila called her sister and Maneck was around to say Happy New Year. They were with their four children which made Mala happy.

Sharon spoke to her mum, who was on the other side of town with all of her AA friends.

And Noor was at a table with… strangers.

The streets were filled with people. It was freezing cold when Sharon and Mala started walking.

Sophia and Dave had enough of the English pomposity at the hotel, so they too decided to take a walk down the street.

Noor and Ahmed felt like trapped children with his parents so they too decided to leave.

Dave was so inspired by London again. He was reminiscing about his young gay days when he was at the London Institute of Fashion. He was so young back then. He had some very wild times and met people in the art scenes who taught him the ways of the artistic savant.

Mala held on to Sharon's arm, because the cold was too much for her to bear. She suddenly bolted upright and noticed Noor on the other side of the road. Mala poked Sharon on her side and she too looked up. Their friend was even bigger and Ahmed looked like a trophy. They didn't match at all.

Mala began to walk quicker in their direction and decided to bring out the little Indian Hanuman monkey in her. Or perhaps the little *Krishna*, who was the most mischievous Hindu deity in this atmospheric universe, an ashy blue deity who had cravings for bowls of stolen butter. Mala was definitely trying to reach her bowl of grease.

"Come on *aunty*, let's go!" Mala was pulling Sharon as she spoke.

Mala made a bee line for Noor and stopped right in front of her face. "Hi Noor. Happy New Year."

Noor jumped and wobbled all at the same time. She was surprised. "Hi Mala, how are you? And Sharon... Happy New Year."

"Aren't you going to introduce us to your new boyfriend, Noor?" Mala asked as she put her hand out graciously to shake Ahmed's hand. "I'm Mala, and this is Sharon."

He didn't shake her hand; he pushed his hair back, looked behind her to scope the scene and said, "The pleasure is all mine." His distance was so cliché and ugly. Sharon could see right through his complicated, untrustworthy demeanour.

"Annabelle, I think we should go now. This isn't really our scene. Nice to meet you ladies," Ahmed said as he started walking away.

Noor was right behind him, waddling like the nurse from Franco Zepherelli's *Romeo and Juliet*. Mala wanted to scream, 'a sail... a sail...' but thought the wiser.

As soon as Ahmed and Noor got around the corner he let go of her arm. "Who were those girls? They look so trashy and loose..." Ahmed was talking with his hands. "The short elf one... the red head one looks so rough around the edges... and the other one is so strange. She speaks with such a funny accent. What is she? Indian? Pakistani? Persian? Latina? Did you used to be like them?"

Noor was nervous; she could feel knots in her stomach and feel like she could be losing something again. She didn't want the same incident as a week before where she was left all alone at her father's.

"Did you used to be like them Annabelle?" Ahmed demanded with more force.

Noor hesitated, "Not exactly."

"Well, be glad that you are with me now. I'll show you the right way." He said as he began to walk away from her again.

"And what is that! Leaving me alone while you go out for your so-called business dinners and not calling for hours? Is that what you want to teach me?" Annabelle started to yell, stopping Ahmed in his tracks. You could see his face start to scrunch up from the interior as he began to bite the insides of his cheeks.

"Where do you think money comes from? The sky? It's not easy to make money. You know that right?" he said coming closer to her like a poised cobra about to pounce.

"And what has that got to do with you not calling me the other night? Or the other morning?"

"I was at a business meeting Annabelle."

"Until 6 a.m.?"

"I was home at 2 a.m." Guilt was starting to crescendo up the creep's face.

"No, you weren't." Annabelle was coming closer to Ahmed now. She looked like a mother cobra ready to spit her venom.

"How do you know? Did you follow me?" He turned around and grabbed her by the shoulders. "Did you? Because if you don't trust me there is no point in us…"

"Ouch Ahmed, you are hurting me," she yelped. He was strong and very rough.

He let go of her fiercely and said. "I don't need this insecurity game." He started to walk away from her again, but this time his pace was much faster. Noor looked back to see if her *best girls* were there, but they were nowhere to be found or seen in an ocean of different people all around.

The same time that Ahmed and Noor had turned the corner and had their little tiff, both Sharon and Mala knew that they had to rescue their friend.

"We have to save her, Sharon."

"Not today precious."

"When?"

"Soon, my love, soon."

Sophia stayed the night at Dave's hotel. They woke up in the afternoon and had breakfast on the terrace. It was cold, but the view overlooking Hyde Park was sensational. It was Dave's idea to sit outside because he needed to rest his eyes. He said everything in Hong Kong was in such close proximity to everything else. Looking out any flat window would definitely garner a scene of some Chinese man in his tight, white speedo underwear probably doing *tai chi*. It was gruesome to watch but not today. Dave was in London and he was going to stay for five more days. He wanted to shop and visit some of his old haunts.

Dave pushed his plate to the side and began to talk about Craig. He had called Dave and had confessed how much he missed Sophia. He knew exactly what he was like. Not like her former boyfriends who were either bankrupt, homophobic, or sexist. Craig was actually in love with Sophia. She revealed that she had nothing to say to him anymore and was unsure what to think in regards to the incident with the white Tai Tai.

"Nothing in this life is an accident…"

Sophia rolled her eyes.

"You promised you wouldn't interrupt Sophia," Dave said like a stern father.

"I didn't say anything Dave."

"Facial expressions count. So stop rolling your eyes, I can hear your eyeballs gurgling around. Anywayyyyssss, nothing in this life is an accident, and everything happens for a reason. Sometimes we have to go on a voyage to take a breather, and then come back to our place we call home. When we come full circle, we will reach some kind of conclusion. That doesn't mean to say going through the cycle will be easy; it might be difficult sometimes but the obstacles and tests put in our way are not meant to hurt, but rather to enhance..."

"Enhance what?" Sophia interrupted.

"Upppp uppppp uuupppp... I'm not finished yet. Some of us wonder, like you, Sophia why do we have to go through all these tests, if there is a God. You know and I know we are very lucky. We have everything right?"

"Yes," she said almost rolling her eyes again.

"So, I leave you with one thought. There is no need to answer, or question, it is not meant for the purpose of a debate. What I'm about to say to you, is for you to ponder. Okay?"

"Okay Dave..." Sophia was getting bored. He was getting into lecture mode, and she was feeling drained.

"There is no need to wonder about the white Tai Tai or Craig or Alister or your father. This is for you alone."

"Hurry up Dave!"

"Don't rush me petal, I want this to be a poignant moment."

"Oh God!" She leaned her head back to look at the beautiful wintery blue sky, augmented with a chilly steam in the air; which seemed to cascade like a blue mist across the atmosphere.

"Yes Sophia. *Oh God* is right, which leads me into exactly what I want to say." He made a dramatic pause, cleared his throat like a cliché drama queen and said. "If God brings you *to* it, then he will bring you *through* it."

Sophia began laughing hysterically. Dave looked at her and smiled back at his friend. "You will know, petal, what this means one day."

"I'm sure Dave," Sophia said with stinging sarcasm.

"Don't be so cynical. God does help us in times of need... and maybe He will direct you back to your *original* place..."

"Okay. Okay Dave... no more religion talk..."

They both sat on the terrace the whole afternoon drinking champagne, eating breakfast and more breakfast and some more lunch, until it got so cold the universe forced them back inside.

Sophia made her way back to Surrey and giggled at the thought of her going back to her original place... Asia... There was no way she would even consider it. Not in a million years.

"Max stop that! Mummy is very upset with you. Stop bullying Josie! OW!" Max was so hyper to see Sophia and was jumping on top of Josie, scratching her father's furniture. When Sophia told him off, he pounced on her and scratched her by accident. She was glad she was facing the computer.

"That's it, you're going outside!" She picked him up and threw him gently into the garden. Max didn't like the outdoors. He detested it, because of his Asian house cat attitude – spoilt, snobbish and homebound. He began to meow like a lost, stray cat. Sophia ignored him and checked her emails. Six new ones. She deleted three and read the other three.

From: Alister Martin

Hey sis, thanks so much for the PlayStation games. My eyes are glued to the TV. Can't stop playing. Loving the WAR GAMES.

Alister.

From: Margaret Martin

Dear Sophia,

Merry Christmas Sweetheart. I wasn't home when you rang. I've been on holiday. To Indonesia. It was amazing. I spoke to Alister, he seems fine. He told me you were with your dad. Give him my regards.

Love You.

Mum

From: **Craig Matthews**

She wanted to delete his message, but for some reason, a force, or something that pushed her, made her open up the email.

Dearest Sophia,

I know how much you hate soppy scenarios, but I needed to write to you. To get a few issues off my chest. I was... AM... a coward for not calling when you told me your plans regarding your move to London. My ex, Jennifer, decided to surprise me and my life became a bit of a shambles. I have nothing to do with her anymore, and rest assured, it is over between me and her. I would have liked to have remain friends with her, but she drove me round the bend while she was here. The entire time I was thinking about you. Distance is difficult, especially with you. I know you are cringing at this part. I can see your face all bunched up and your mouth crooked to the side and your eyes in a squint.

Sophia caught her reflection on the screen and quickly resumed a *normal* face expression.

It is such a shame we didn't find each other sooner. I want you to know that meeting you has finally made me see, at my age, that you made me realize what I have been looking for in a relationship. I hope you will write soon... even if it's just to say hello. I know I hurt you. If I could change the way you feel, and turn back time, I would indeed do it this second.

I remain,

Graciously yours,

Craig

Sophia felt so bad for him. He was besotted by her. Maybe she should have felt flattered, but she just wasn't wholeheartedly interested. She did think about writing back to him, but she really had nothing to say. She was going to follow her instincts, like Dave told her, and wait for a *sign*.

She forwarded the email to Dave.

From: Sophia Martin

Dear Dave,

Missing you already… look at what Craig has gotten himself into.

Love you,

Sophia

She rested her eyes from the computer and went into the kitchen to make a cup of tea. She suddenly realised that she had forgotten about Max outside in the cold. She hurriedly opened the veranda door and let him in. He leaped on her like a dog and placed his big fat head on her shoulders. His meowing and purring was like an extension of her hearing. It was like music for her, a familiar sound and echo, a language not of her own, letting her know she was never alone.

Chapter 24

London

School started and the New Year brought renewal, new shifts and some overweight students back into her classroom. Mala was talking to Simran, a pudgy Indian girl with a thick Bangladeshi accent, who had the mouth and demeanour of a 62 year old Indian woman. Her environment was a true reflection of her upbringing.

Simran was talking about her Christmas vacation. She was giving a presentation for Speech Day, something Mala instituted to help and foster confidence for public speaking. They had just moved to London six months ago and the little third grader was doing very well adjusting to life away from her grandmother's home in India. Both her parents had moved first and made enough money to bring Simran back with them last year.

"So, Simran, thank you for volunteering to speak first on Speech Day. Can you please tell us what you will be talking about today?"

"My mahmah tole me that I should buy her a samosa machine for Christmas. Because every time there is a Christmas party I alvays put up hand and tell teacher I vill bring samosa. So I vant to know vhere I can buy a samosa machine for her… and I also tole her vhen I grow up I vant to be British so I can bring pizzzaaaa to school." Simran said shaking her head from side to side as she punctuated all the z's in the word "pizza." The other students giggled at her hand movements and head shaking and her absolutely animated Bollywood explanation of her samosa machine. Mala was giggling inside.

"That was a wonderful story Simran. Thank you. Now, who's next?" Mala asked. The whole class put up their hands with eager delight. They were so bright. She loved it. She looked at Timmy. He was from Brixton, and his parents had found out he was a genius when he was three years old. He was gifted in math, played the violin and he could read high level books. They sent him to a Montessori School, so he could be more sociable. They invested a lot of money in their son. He was an introvert on the playground, and when other people talked to him, he would look away, pointing his ear at them, to ensure they knew he was listening.

Eye contact was a challenge for Timmy; however, occasionally, he would look into Mala's eyes. He had the most glorious blue eyes Mala had ever seen. They were deep and sincere and full of questions as well as knowledge. He had a very strong inner city London accent. Timmy walked onto the dark army green carpet and pulled down his shirt. Mala could see he was nervous. He looked to the side, at first, facing the window.

"So, Timmy can you tell us about your Christmas vacation?"

"*I goh a bye see kal, and it's mauuf...*"

"I see, wow that's a beautiful colour Timmy. Can you tell the class what mauve is?"

"*Yeah... it's red and... blue like and it's me favourite colour... because it's opposite... and me Dah says opposites attract. So I fink tha if redan blue are attracted to each ofher... then thas me kind of attraction... and I was attracted to the bike. I rode it on Boxin' Day with me Dah. It was lots of fun.*"

"Thank you Timmy. I really enjoyed your story."

"*Fank you Ms. Mala. For enjoyin' me story,*" Timmy said as he smiled to the window and walked back to his seat.

It took the whole morning to listen to all her students' stories collected from the holidays. They brought magic, excitement and true raw inspiration into her life. She loved her job. She wished, only sometimes, that she had made a decision to have children when she was younger. Her peak point for child bearing days was past. She reminisced about her childhood and how her mother looked with her swollen belly when she was about to have Mila. Mala thought about what she needed to do, whether to contact her mother... or not. She turned around to scope her classroom and realised that she was happy she wasn't a parent. She never wanted to turn out like hers. A stabbing pain in her heart made her feel so guilty for thinking of her parents in that way. She couldn't help it. She wished she could let go and think of a way she could do better.

At exactly 3:30 p.m., Sharon called her. "*Aunty*, Noor called. Meet me at Bazica in 20 minutes. This is the day we are going to save her, precious."

"No harsh words, okay Sharon. If we are going to save her, we need to make sure we don't drown her with too many words."

When Mala got there, she saw Ahmed sitting in her seat. She knew Sharon was going to disapprove of this scene. She hoped she wouldn't come in like a scowling director, insisting that everyone listen to her.

Mala started to breathe and think of Master Kamal's techniques for a better and clearer image. Fatima was not in the café today. Mala wished she was so she could finally see the three friends reunited. Minus Ahmed of course.

Mala greeted Ahmed and Noor, and gave her a big bear hug. One thing Noor had the ability to do, was to forgive quickly. It came across as uncaring and a little bit two faced, but she did have the ability to move forward quickly.

Ahmed was staring up and down at Mala. He thought she looked stunning today. She was in her work clothes and was glowing from Speech Day.

When Sharon walked in, her heart dropped. Noor gave her an equally affectionate bear hug when she walked in.

The four of them made boring small talk. Mala tried her best to make Ahmed comfortable, but it wasn't working. His sharp, curt and overly edgy conversation, not to mention his one word answers, made the atmosphere tense.

"So, Ahmed what do you do? What is your line of work?" Mala inquired.

"I work for myself," Ahmed replied without any eye contact.

"Oh that's good. Doing what?" Mala asked with true inquiry.

"Making money." Ahmed was smirking. "What is this, a court of law?"

"No sweetheart, she was just asking..." Noor said touching Ahmed's shoulders in a very patronizing manner.

He looked over at Mala and said, "Banking... and what is your line of work Ms. Amani?"

"I'm a teacher." She smiled with confidence.

"I see. That's nice..." He looked at Annabelle. "I have to go now. I don't want to ruin your afternoon. I will meet you back at your flat later." He got up and waved with his back turned as he left.

"Isn't he cute?" Noor asked as she dreamily watched him leave Bazica with his arrogant pants on.

"Stunning," Sharon said with deep and meaningful sarcasm, as she dragged harshly on her cigarette.

"I wanted to say I am so sorry for my behaviour the other night when we bumped into each other on the road. I was very rude... and I want you to be my bridesmaids." Noor was squeaking by the end of her sentence.

"Who are you marrying?" Sharon asked with circles of smoke emanating from her lips.

"Ahmed of course. And both of you have to be there. Please. I need you there. I will call you tonight and fill you in on all the details." She squeezed both of her friend's hands and got up to pay for the bill.

"I thought this was the day we were supposed to save her? We aren't doing a very good job are we?" Mala whispered to Sharon as Noor walked back.

She hugged her friends and Noor left Bazica.

"Wow, well that was a head spin. That guy is a twat. He is going to ruin her some more. I'm so worried about her." Sharon went off into her Indian aunty voice... "First *Pitaji's restaurant, then a book, now a marriage. Vot is going on yar!*" Sharon was shaking her head from side to side with her fiery red hair, which looked like an ignition to her thoughts.

Mala was laughing. "Just wish her well."

"I will, I promise not to rain on her parade. I guess she is happy, she looks happy. Maybe you were right, she's happy in her own life. That's why she never calls." Sharon took out another cigarette as she spoke. Mala hastily grabbed it from her hand and gave her the death stare.

When Mala and Sharon got home, they were excited for Noor and her prospect of marriage and decided to wait patiently for her phone call.

They didn't hear from her for another six months.

"I don't want you associating with them!" Ahmed was playing with his hair furiously.

"Why Ahmed?" Noor was in tears again. It wasn't supposed to be like this. "They are my friends." She felt so menopausal all the time. Maybe she needed to go and see a doctor or check her hormones. Or was it that she was always attracting negative forces, banging against her true self?

"Stop it Annabelle! You are such a nuisance when you cry like that. And stop asking why? Why? Like a big baby. They are not our calibre. They are not like you."

"I've known them for so long. We practically grew up together, since our freshman days at college. Do you know how long that is?" Noor had flashbacks of their college days. It seemed like so long ago. Where had her life taken her? What was she doing? Wasting her precious life away.

"They are not in the same category as you. It's me or them. You decide. I can't have a high life like this, and have riff raff for friends. It doesn't match my stigma or my stance."

'Stigma?' Noor thought. What an awkward word to use on yourself. Did he mean enigma? He really was a stigma… a sore one too.

"And another thing Annabelle, all those emails from the *sailor*… erase them or I'll do it for you…"

"How do you know about that… and how do you know he's a sailor…?" Annabelle was stunned.

"I have my ways Annabelle Noor… I have my ways." Ahmed was peering at her like a hawk.

Noor was scared.

Sophia was getting restless; it was almost February and she still hadn't found a job. She didn't really need it, because of her earnings in Asia. She just needed to do something to feel productive and feel like there was movement in her brain and in her cellular and molecular structure. She was aging, but not enough that she couldn't get out of bed and feel like she was important. Even a part time job would suffice for her. She opened the classified section of the newspaper and all she could see was an ocean of ads for teaching jobs. She turned the page. Finance, banking, more banking, finance, marketing, PR. She didn't know what she wanted to do with her life. She was in the perfect setting. Now all she needed to do was find the perfect job to keep her mind working.

She strolled into the kitchen and made herself some breakfast. She found it so much easier to wake up in England. The fresh air, the winter greenery, the cool breeze and no Alister strumming wildly and rambunctiously on his guitar at six in the morning after a gig. Thank God she was always awake at that time. The stock markets and numbers were already swimming around in her head every morning at five thirty. His music was always a wakeup call through melody; constructed by formulas and numbers to create a vibration, a tone, a sound. She missed her brother tremendously. Nevertheless, she sensed that she needed her space today. She hadn't heard from Dave in two weeks. He was probably busy with Sergio. His new love interest. A fashion intern from LVMH. He was very cute. Dave always fell in love so easily, and on many occasions suffered severe boredom from routine. Hopefully, Sergio would teach him that routine and repetition was sometimes healing for the soul.

Mala was getting ready for Washington to leave. He had been invited to Cannes to play at a wedding. His clothes were strewn all over the living room and his instruments were scattered around the flat.

"Help me Mala, I'm going to miss my flight. Please baby. I got back from La Bella Luna so late last night." Washington was brushing his teeth and speaking with a pink towel wrapped around his waist. Mala had bought him a set of blue towels. But he never understood the purpose of differentiation – his and hers. He needed to get dry and whatever colour towel was available, he would use it.

Mala was frustrated and tired. She had known that he might get this amazing gig in Cannes, but it was so sudden, and he confirmed in such haste. He was so excited. "I don't know what you want to pack." She sounded annoyed. "Why do you always leave everything to the last minute?"

"I was working Mala."

"I work too Washington."

"I have to make money my dear," he said from the bathroom. He was getting agitated. "Please just help me finish packing and don't be in a sour mood with me. I am leaving. Alex is coming to pick me up in twenty minutes. Please." He walked back into the bathroom.

Alex was one of Washington's band members and he was also like an extension of their family.

Mala stopped packing and looked in his direction. She was looking at his back. His muscles were protruding out and his back looked so strong and fierce. "You are leaving for three weeks and this is how you say goodbye to me? By asking me to pack your things? All you ever do is think about yourself Washington. When do you ever think about me? You come home at God knows what time, and I wait for you, cook for you, am here for you…"

He interrupted, "I do things for you too. So please don't start with me."

"Who do you think you are Mr. Cannelli? You are one of the most selfish people I have ever met in my life."

He ignored her and walked away into the bedroom with a very grouchy look on his face. He didn't want to deal with this right now. He was about to leave London.

"Why are you walking away from me? And why aren't you listening to me? I know what it is… you are having an affair right? Is that why you are going to Cannes, because of all the beautiful women there? Is it?" Mala caught herself, she was going too far. She sounded like an adolescent. My goodness, she thought. How harsh. And so far from her truthful thoughts. What was she thinking? She was picking a fight with him because she didn't want him to go anywhere.

He didn't answer her. He began to think of the divine melody in his head. But she kept talking and turning the melodic notes, in his mind, to a stinging whining sound.

He was upset. "If this is the way you want to see me off, then so be it. Be like that." He wasn't interested in arguing anymore. And her assumption of him having an affair was ludicrous. He didn't even want to begin to justify himself.

"I'm serious Washington." She walked into their bedroom. He was spraying deodorant all over his body and around himself.

He was calm. "I don't know why you are saying these things."

"Get a real job Washington." She knew she was hurting him some more. "It's been years and we live in sin... you never think about marriage and if I could have changed my life path maybe I would have had children, and in the not so distant future, I would have had grandchildren."

With even more calmness and stature like a grand Pharaoh he looked at Mala and said, "We will see when the time comes."

"Is that why you have me here hanging around? To still see if you want me when the time comes?"

"Mala, stop this nonsense. Please baby, please." He was looking directly at her as he pulled his shirt over her head.

"You never give me a straight answer. I want to get married one day. I am not getting any younger." Mala stormed out of the room and continued to pack his suitcase in a disorderly fashion; throwing clothes inside the suitcase like a typhoon.

Her back was turned to Washington and he could see that she was very upset. Being twelve years older than her always made him feel like he had to protect Mala. He smiled without her seeing and said, "I love you. You know that right?"

She didn't turn around to face him; she was still throwing clothes and instruments into his bag in a jumbled mess. "I don't know if you really love me. Sometimes I think you love your bongos and your friends more than me. I don't want to talk about this anymore."

"I agree. Alex will be here in ten minutes. I don't want to fight with you. You know that this gig is going to bring in a lot of money for us. Maybe even fame."

Mala sat on the sofa after her tumultuous packing session and sulked. She didn't want to argue with him. She wanted more of a commitment from him. He never talked about marriage with her or a solid future with her. He loved to live in the moment. She thought about Noor and for a split second and thought how lucky she is.

"You know what, Noor is getting married."

"Ahhhhhhhhhhh… so, this is what this is about." He said circling his arms around the air. "There is no rush princess. We will do it when the time is right for us."

"What if the time is now Washington?"

"Like, right this minute?" he asked putting more socks in his bag.

"No Washington. I am being serious. Can you please stop and look at me when I'm talking to you?"

He stopped, looked at her and said, "There is a time and place for everything and everyone."

"Then why isn't it our turn yet? Do I have to be a hundred year old woman before you ask me to marry you?"

He turned to zip up his bag. "Money."

"You are so materialistic Washington! How can love be about money? They are not the same thing."

"Listen, please don't get angry again. We need money to get married. We need money to live comfortably. I do not want us to live hand to mouth. We need money to pay the bills. Love doesn't pay for the heating when it's cold." Washington was smiling.

"I really don't find any of this amusing."

"Do you want to get married? Mala."

"YES. I. DO." Mala's Indian eyes were bulging angrily out of her face.

"Okay, then we will very soon," he said as he wrapped his big strong hands around Mala and hugged her tightly. He smelled so good. She really didn't want him to leave. "I love you princess. I will call you as soon as I get there. And don't worry about anything."

"The only thing we don't need to let us know that we are married, is a piece of paper."

"Yes we do."

"Then we will get one, so you can hang it up on the wall next to our pictures in the spare room."

"Don't mock me Washington."

The buzzer rang, it was Alex.

"I will call you, okay my love." He cupped Mala's face in his hands and kissed her passionately. "Ride the lazy wave princess. It's much calmer."

Mala half smiled at him. He picked up his things and left the flat.

Chapter 25

South East Asia

Craig was feeling depleted. He was beginning to abhor Hong Kong. Sophia was right. He still couldn't get her out of his mind. Chinese New Year was coming and that meant one week of nothingness. So many Asian cities with Chinese descendants would be closed for fifteen days. Nothing was in operation; banks, shops, supermarkets, shopping malls and schools all closed.

Craig was depressed. He didn't want to spend another New Year on his own, be it English, American, Chinese, Singaporean, or Yugoslavian. He had spent the last holiday getting drunk and watching TV on his own. He needed a real holiday. He could hear most of the people in his office talk about exotic holidays; they had already planned for Chinese New Year.

Loretta was going to the Maldives with her husband and three kids. Kim was going to the Thai island of Koh Samui with her boyfriend. Even Kitty was going abroad – dubbed Hello Kitty because of all the cat carnage of pink and white all over her desk. Once, she wrote a memo to Stan, the big boss, on Hello Kitty paper and he almost fired her. She could not stop talking to her friends in a very loud Cantonese accent about her "shopping and eating trip to Taipei." How very mundane and consciously unenlightening. She did the same tour package every year.

Craig looked at his computer. One new email. It was from Sophia. He was so excited, he wondered why he didn't notice it before. He started to say 'Thank you, thank you, thank you.' He had no idea who he was thanking, but it was obvious why he was suddenly in high spirits.

From: Sophia Martin

Wanted to drop you a line to say "hello."

Sophia.

He typed back right away.

From: Craig Matthews – *CITIBANK*

Sophia, so happy to hear from you. Are you well? How is your father? Max? Josie?

He paused; he didn't know what else to write… and then… something inspired him…

Chinese New Year is coming up. There's a lot of hype and excitement. Especially in my office. Everyone is going away to have a "break." I'll be in London for ten days. I have asked Stan for a few extra days off from my annual leave.

He was lying, but he was going to get on it as soon as he finished writing to her.

My mother and father have asked me to visit them.

Another white lie but he was going to call them ASAP.

Hope we can meet up for a coffee or a drink when I get there.

Take care,

Craig

He clicked the send button and proceeded to call his mother and father, his travel agent and the HR manager to arrange for a few extra days off.

Alister was lying on his bed strumming his out of tune guitar. He hadn't showered, eaten, slept or spoken to anyone in four days.

Chapter 26

London

Mala was *loofa-ing* her body with vanilla milkshake washing foam. The suds smelled like pudding. She washed her hair and put a treatment in it so it would retain its shine. At least, that's what the packaging promised. After her beautiful cleansing and washing away of all the grime of the day, week and the month, Mala felt like a shiny happy person.

She got out of the shower smelling like a fragrant flower that smelled like dessert. Sweet, yet tender, soft and willowy, with the scent lingering for a few seconds… not musky, not flowery, just the right amount of spritz to feel like the summer sun was always on your shoulder.

Washington had already been gone a week and surprisingly, she hadn't missed him as much as she thought she would. She was loving her space and the lack of cluster. Mala was a bit of a perfectionist and she liked her flat tidy. She hated mess. She would occasionally bark at Washington when he didn't help. His 'long hours' stopped working as an excuse.

She was towel drying her hair when the buzzer rang. She wasn't expecting anyone. She threw on her bathrobe – pink with powder blue sea shells. She answered the door. Someone cleared their voice. It was a man. "Is this Mala Amani?"

"Yes."

"Can we come up please?"

Mala was mildly frightened, and she asked curtly, "Who is this?"

"We are from Forsythe and Collins, the London branch…"

That name sounded familiar.

"We have been asked to locate your whereabouts, Ms. Amani."

"Can you give me a moment? Actually right now is not an appropriate time."

"We are sorry to bother you Ms. Amani. However, we do need to speak to you in person. It's rather urgent."

Mala threw on a pair of jeans and an old sweater. She looked like a young 30 year old… or maybe not… wishful thinking maybe. She threw the ugly sweater over her head and flung it on the floor. She put a light green collared shirt on instead. She looked in the mirror. She looked much better. More decent. "Sorry to keep you waiting. Please come up." She pressed the button so hard, it broke and kept on buzzing. "Shoot! Shoot! Shoot!" She was screaming at herself with the plastic end of the buzzer still in her fingers.

As the men began ascending the stairs, Mala went into the kitchen, got a large knife and used it as a lever to unblock the buzzer. It finally stopped by itself.

She opened the door and two distinguished lawyer-type men in immaculate attire stood in the doorway. Mala was still holding the knife.

"Hello Ms. Amani, nice to make your acquaintance. Sorry to disturb you." He put out his hand to shake hers and she obliged. I'm Robert McConnohay and this is Leonard Sticks. We are both from Forsythe and Collins. May we come in?" Robert was doing all the talking as Leonard stared at Mala like she was from the movie *Psycho*. His eyes pierced hers and she looked down at her hand. She slowly put the knife down.

"Um… yes please come in … it's not what you think… I was fixing the buzzer… please, please come in and have a seat. Would you like anything to drink?" Mala was a bit shaky in her throat when she spoke. She could feel a vibration of sky blue and a dark navy blue float in the back of her throat. She didn't know whether to scream or whisper.

The two men came in and asked for a cup of tea. They sat at the dining table in a very formal manner as Mala graciously walked into the kitchen. She began talking to herself.

'Breathe Mala breathe... don't worry, they are here for a reason... they better not tell me that Santosh has risen from the dead! ...breathe... green light, yellow light... no... think golden. Golden light...'

She was breathing heavily as she brewed the tea and calmly returned to the men in her living room.

Ms. Amani, we have been asked to give you these papers following your father's death." He handed her a folder. "Inside you will see a series of documents that need your signature. It is for reclaiming his fortune, which will be divided equally between you and your younger sister."

Mala took the folder; she didn't know what to do with it. Simultaneously, Leonard took out an extra copy of her folder. "If you turn to page 4, 6, 9, 12, 18, 22, 28, 29, 30 and 32, you will see that your signature is required in the spaces we have indicated with an arrow." Mala couldn't remember all the page numbers, but she opened the first page and felt like crying.

"Is there anything else I can do for you gentlemen?" Mala said looking down at all the paper in front of her.

"We would like to go through the paper work with you, if you have time."

"I'm actually on my way to another very important meeting... engagement." She wasn't, but she wanted these men out of her home. She cleared her throat and with dignity as well as grace said, "So, right now I can't, but if you give me a few days to review the documents..."

Leonard, who was much younger and feistier than Robert, interrupted Mala and said. "When do you think you will have these documents ready Ms. Amani?"

"In a few days, if you leave your business card, then I can drop it off to your office… *and…*"

Leonard interrupted again, "Do you think tomorrow would be possible?"

Mala was very annoyed at Leonard and his audacity to speak to her so curtly in her house; and for disrespecting her at her age. She stopped and wondered if she was really thinking like a true *aunty*. She was. She had three nieces and one nephew. She decided to put on her best *aunty* front and speak to Leonard like he deserved.

"Mr. Sticks, that is your name right? I am busy at the moment, and like I said, I need a few days to look over the documents. And when I'm done and have read it thoroughly and with ease, only then will I give you a call."

Leonard looked away like a sullen puppy. Robert on the other hand was calm and smiled at Mala; they were on the same page. "We understand," he said, "Please take your time and be in touch. Here is my business card." Robert boldly handed over his card, while Leonard sheepishly tucked his hand into his inside suit pocket and handed his card to Mala with a little boy's face.

They both got up to leave and Mala was left alone with Santosh's financial history. She threw it on the sofa, and decided to deal with it the next day. She craved for Washington's warmth, music and presence.

That night when she went to bed, she dreamt of her father.

He was wearing a white robe like a *swami* and he was teaching a group of children about *samsara* and *nirvana*. He was articulating something, but Mala couldn't hear him. She felt like he was saying he would always be there for them. Suddenly he was on a boat, taking these children down a silver lined river. In the river were sparkles of sapphires. His mouth was moving, but she couldn't hear what he was saying. Finally after a golden mist escaped his lips, he became audible. Powder blue glitter emanated from his mouth as diamonds cascaded from his fingertips. He explained that the river was the flow of life, and with guidance one would obtain the skills and patience to row down the river with ease. His voice echoed in her mind. It was the same voice he used when he read her favourite book to her – *Animal Daddies and My Daddy*. He said, "With proper guidance and the right direction, we can all reach this river we call *samsara*. If we can grasp the idea with full force, we will find *nirvana* in no time."

The dream suddenly and sharply changed course, into a different paradigm, or a past one, that was uncomfortable and murky. He was standing in their house, in the living room, in San Francisco. He was talking to Mala and telling her how much he loved her. He told her she was a good girl and she was going to be fine. Suddenly, he climbed onto a desk and a rope fell from the ceiling. With a very dangerous smile, he put the rope around his neck and jumped off the table.

The picture in her mind changed and the face became her mother's.

Mala woke up sweating and shaking. She was lost in her old subconscious. She wanted to cry, scream and shake the earth. She picked up the phone but didn't know who to call. She put the receiver back down again and looked at the clock by her bedside. It was 4:44 a.m. She called her sister.

They spoke on the phone for half an hour and Mala informed Mila that the lawyers would probably be contacting her soon. Mala revealed to her sister that she wasn't sure if she wanted to speak to their mother, and said she was still wondering what to do with the papers she had thrown on the sofa the night before. After a long silence, the sisters bid each other farewell and Mala picked up the folder... all of it was so complicated. She signed each line indicated to her with post it notes. She hardly read any of it. She didn't quite know what she was doing. All she knew is that she really did miss her mother.

Later that morning, she dropped the papers to Forsythe and Collins on Fleet Street and handed the documents over to Robert's secretary.

She left the big building and walked in the smog; the air was thick and heavy. The only thing stopping her from contacting her was her relationship with Washington, and the stigma attached to his ethnicity and nationality. She didn't want to choose between them. It would be more than hurtful and would simply break her apart if she had to suffer loosing Washington or her mother. Again. She longed for her.

She walked all the way to Chinatown to see Sharon after she finished her teaching day. When she got about three blocks away from the school, she saw a Chinese lady sitting on an old brown stool. She was wearing a beautiful *cheung sum* made of pink silk, and emerald green flowers trimmed with golden thread. She was talking to a deck of ten by ten cards. "*Yut ee saam, say, mm, lok, yut, yut, yut…*"

Mala walked closer to her. The cards were decorated with ornate Chinese characters. Each character was made with gold leaf paper, and the border had scarlet sequins carefully placed around the whole card. She turned around sharply to Mala and was semi shouting at her.

"*Wah you wan hah?*"

"Nothing." Mala was a bit confused. She didn't think she was bothering the little old Chinese lady in any way.

"*I not sell anything go!… Go… Go!*" she was waving her hands furiously as she tried to usher Mala out of the way, her thick Cantonese accent piercing the grey air every time she opened her mouth to speak.

"*Lo!*" She put the cards behind her back. "*Only if you have a reason… you look lah!… Otherwise… Go… go… go…*"

Her Pidgin English wasn't making Mala scared. Instead, it made her smile. She loved being in London. It reminded her of a painting where everything blended in together, like the Sistine Chapel. Yet, when one looked at each figure carefully, one could see that every single one was completely different and enchantingly unique.

"I'm sorry, I didn't mean to offend you. Your cards are beautiful," Mala said as she stepped back from the old lady's space.

"*Wah you wan... hah?*"

"Why are you sitting out here in the open? It's so cold."

"*No cole... Northern China... vely cole.*"

"May I sit down?" Mala was interested in this old lady, so she tried to sit down.

"*Loh... loh... you go! Go lah...*" She put the cards behind her back again.

Mala laughed. "Would you like a coffee?"

"*Lo, Chinese lo drink coffee... In China only tea... jasmine tea... In China we like tea.*" She paused, stared at Mala and waved her index finger in her face, and grunted. "*Same like India. Many... many... many tea in India.*"

"Yes," Mala said looking at the lines embedded in her face. Her forehead had many creases. Her wrinkles resonated lines of speeches, monologues and distant dialogues she had with loved ones. Each indentation on her soft face reminded Mala of a river, carrying the ebb and flow of history. Stories from afar and tales to match the present. She began to deal her cards on the hard, cold cemented ground. Her wrinkled hands showed signs of a very multifaceted story. Flecks of liver spots spattered in different places, and lime green veins protruded out of her delicate Chinese hands.

"*You look.*"

Mala looked at her.

"*Lo! Lot me... here... here... girl-o... here...*" Her gaze was piercing yet tender. She poked the ground with her fragile finger as she spoke.

"*Wah you see?*"

"Beautiful writing."

"And wah else?"

"Gold, red, black…"

"Lo! Lo… you look more."

Mala bent down towards the cards and on the bottom left hand corner she saw numbers: 1, 14, 16, 28, and 24. She didn't quite understand what was going on, and was freaking out a bit. She had shivers down her back as one of the cards caught her attention. The glare of the adorned red sequins shone into her almond eyes like a dragon's fire.

"What does this card mean? My best friend gave me a card that had this number on it," Mala picked up the 44 card.

"Wah… this say die… die… You tell your friend… this is die die. 44 is die die… aiyaaaaaaa…"

Mala felt a lump in her throat again. A big ball of tightness. She felt like she needed to vomit. "Die? Die?" She enquired.

"You scare… you lo scare… because I tell you, lo scare… Chinese people say is vely vely bad number. They say no lucky… no good… no good."

"Really?"

"No good lah… no good lah…"

"I have to go now." Mala tried to get up. She didn't want any more of it. She wanted to stop believing in all these superstitions. Colours, numbers and signs. The old lady interrupted her chaotic thoughts…

"Lo… you… lo go."

"I have to," Mala said, as she placed her hands in her pockets. She wasn't going to think anymore. Every time she came across this number 44, she was going to erase it from her mind. She felt cold suddenly… again.

"Wait lah."

"No! I really have to go."

"You no listen… you stubborn girl…"

"Please, I don't mean to be rude… but I have to go home…"

"Whah you have at home…"

Mala thought to herself. Nothing, she had nothing or anyone to go home to. What was she going to do? Sit in the lotus position and conjure up colours for healing and therapy and pretend that the divine powers are always near her? She knew this cynicism was not helping her. Mala looked at her with complete agitation. "What! …I wish I never sat here. I don't want to know anymore please."

"Chinese say 44 is vely bad… but I say vely good."

"That's nice." Mala was inching away from her.

"And you must say 44 is vely vely good."

"No I didn't," Mala said with sarcasm.

"India peoples… vely smart… you… ancient civilisation…" She stood up. She was so short. She had the decorative card in her hand and was waving it in front of her face. *"Wah happens when you die?"*

"You die," Mala said as she began to stand up. She looked like a giant in front of the Chinese lady.

"Lo… lo…"

"Then what?"

"You live you have life."

"What?"

"You die and die… but nobody die… inside death is life…" She sat down again on her little wooden stool and ignored Mala.

"Can you say that again please?"

She wasn't responding to her and began the whole scene from the beginning as life had taken on a karmic moment. She began counting. *"Yut, ee, saam, say, say, say, yut, yut mm, lok, yut…"*

"Excuse me... excuse me..." Mala was desperately trying to get her attention again. But she was not responding. No matter how much Mala tried to converse with her, she reinforced her solitude through ignoring her more and more. Mala felt like Alice from Wonderland, and she had fallen into a Chinatown rabbit hole. Everywhere she looked – on bus stop signs, license plates, post boxes, advertisements, numbers imprinted on drain pipes and road signs, 44 seemed to jump out at her. She quietly decided to embrace the day like climbing up a mountain, trying hard to reach the summit. She tried even harder to comprehend the lawyer's documents.

And like a sign, the universe unravelled itself to her like an intricate Persian carpet. It was like each thread painted a picture for her, explaining her existence on earth, and her interwoven relationships into the fabrics of people's lives. And then without effort or any thought, she stumbled upon an old woman, an ancient Chinese soul who gave her the meaning of everyone's entire existence.

Today she realised that there was more to our everyday routines, fears and thoughts. She felt like there was an eruption in her mind, with all the new information that had bombarded her in the last two days. Sharon was right when she said, 'be careful what you ask for.'

After the lawyer's visit the previous night, she had woken up searching herself, wanting to understand why her life felt like the Grand Prix, racing like lightening in one direction. Did she now have the answers?

Chapter 27

South East Asia

It had been nine days since Tanya broke up with Alister. He couldn't cope. He tried to write a song about her, but all the lyrics were horrible and ugly. He felt like a monster was living inside him. On the sixth day he finally ate a bowl of wonton noodles and tried to call his sister. He needed his sister. His father picked up the phone and he hung up.

His band members were on holiday. They decided to take an earlier Chinese New Year holiday. They asked Alister to join them, but he was in his own world, a land that gave way to a serene landscape; where multicultural flowers bloomed into a conservatory of sleep. The sky was blue, the earth was green, and bright yellow birds sang in the distance. An aquamarine waterfall with flecks of purple fell like a melodic tune, singing in Alister's ear as he slowly drifted far away from his current domain. In his slumber his thoughts moved from a colourful symbolic life, to a murky place, where fire, heat and discomfort dictated his feelings. The name of his demise – Heroin. She was not a lady. She was something that undoubtedly stripped him bare of all of his powers.

Craig was getting ready for his trip. His parents were delighted he was coming home for a few weeks. They didn't ask about Jennifer, which was good. He was going to tell them all about Sophia when he saw them. His parents were very old fashioned and he didn't know if they would accept Sophia. However, he had a strong feeling that they would truly appreciate her kind and warm English manner. Three more days and he would be next to Sophia. He couldn't wait to be near her, and listen to her speak of her family, and her life and listen to the simple pleasures she cherished in her life.

Chapter 28

South East Asia/Surrey

The conversation between brother and sister was so mundane. Nobody could tell who was talking, what was being said, or if anyone was actually being heard. A stranger would have no inclination of what was being communicated between Sophia and Alister, one trying desperately to grasp life and the other not understanding his selfish manic attitudes.

The conversation was like two actors in silhouettes on the stage, throwing lines at each other, with no purpose, recognition or voice. The scene was mundane and unclear.

"Hello."

"How are you?"

"What are you doing?"

"Not much."

"Are you alright?"

"Yes."

"So, what do I owe the pleasure of this phone call?"

"I wanted to say hi."

"That's nice of you."

"How are things there?"

"Fine."

"Sure?"

"Yeah."

"You don't sound very well."

"Just woke up."

"What time is it there?"

"Don't know."

"You don't know what time it is?"

"Dunno."

"Do you know what time it is here?"

"No."

"Something wrong?"

"No."

"Why do you sound so sleepy?"

"Are you my mother?"

"No."

"So, leave me alone."

"What's wrong?"

"Nothing."

"You forgot how to construct proper sentences?"

"No."

"So, what's wrong?"

"Nothing."

"Something's wrong. What is it? Hello? Hello?"

The phone went dead.

Sophia tried to call her brother back, but it sounded like the receiver hadn't been put on the handle properly. A rush of worry began to swarm in her stomach, and she felt dizzy. She knew something was wrong with her brother. He didn't sound himself at all. She didn't know if she should tell her father. She slowed her thoughts and decided to call Dave. She frantically dialled his number.

"Hello?"

"Hey petal, are you alright? It is so late. Is everything okay?" Dave was half asleep and when he looked at the clock, it was 3:30 a.m.

"It's Alister," Sophia was crying.

"What's wrong… are you okay? Sunshine? Why are you crying?"

"I don't know what is wrong with him."

Dave puffed up his pillow and sat straight up in bed. Sergio was beside him snoring like an old man. "Listen petal, calm down."

"He sounded strange Dave."

"How?"

"Really not himself."

"Did you call him back?"

"Yes… but…" Sophia was crying so much on the phone.

Dave's heart sank. "Don't cry like that petal… please be calm… breathe… maybe you are worried for no reason."

Sophia sat on the futon in her father's living room. She was trembling. She knew that addiction was a very demonic power in his life. And he was prone to immersed depression. He needed her, but she was on the other side of the world.

"Dave, please help me… can you please go over there? I know it's so much to ask, but can you please…"

"Don't say any more petal," Dave interrupted. "I will go check on him now."

"Thank you! Thank you… thank you so much! Please call me as soon as you see him."

"I will petal. Hang in there." Dave was beginning to get dressed. He didn't want to leave Sergio on his own. He looked so yummy and angelic. Dave wanted to cuddle up to him. Was he falling in love?

He had never heard Sophia breakdown in the manner he witnessed a few minutes ago. He was definitely baffled. She must have heard something in Alister's voice to have bawled like a lost child. Dave began to worry as well.

When he got to Sophia's old flat he couldn't believe his eyes. The sight he witnessed was tragic. Dave couldn't recognise anything, not even Alister.

He picked Alister up from all the physical mess around him, and brought him back to his flat. On the way back to his home at the Peak, he called Sophia.

"I think you need to see this for yourself."

"Why? Is he okay?" Sophia had panic in her voice.

"No, sunshine he is not. If I were you, I would get over here soon."

"I'll be there tomorrow," Sophia said as she felt her throat and her lips dry up from fright. "Is he going to be okay?"

"Sophia, come back for a few days. I think he really needs you."

The next morning, Sophia packed a small bag and rushed to the airport. She tried to reason with her father that Alister was in dire straits, but he wouldn't listen. He thought Alister was old enough to take care of himself.

"You act like his mother Sophia."

"Dad, please, I know what I am doing."

"If he needs you so much, tell him to move here where we are. So he can be close to family. The bloody idiot has no foundation. And no one to lean on. He is a fool. What kind of person do you think he will progress into… a good for nothing?"

"Whose fault is that Dad?" Sophia asked as she stopped to turn to her father.

"His fault. Hong Kong is a nasty, nasty place. People always fall down there."

"That's not true dad."

""Survival of the fittest Sophia."

"Dad not now please. I will call you when I get there."

Sophia hugged her father, got out of his Jeep and ran to the Cathay Pacific ticket counter. Her flight was leaving in thirty minutes. She bought her ticket and was once again on her way back to South East Asia. She was not herself. She didn't know what she was doing or what was going on. A kaleidoscope of images circled in her mind as pictures of Hong Kong, London, Alister, Dad, Mum and Dave swam around like pieces of a jagged jigsaw trying to find the right fit.

When she landed in the Asian city, Sophia could already feel the demons leap on her shoulder, making her feel tense and stressed. Dave was there to greet her.

"Petal, you look so pale."

"I don't feel like talking right now Dave… I have nothing to say… please take me to my brother."

Sophia felt lost.

Chapter 29

London

Craig was in London with his parents in Hampstead Heath. He sent an email to Sophia, after he confirmed his flight. He got no feedback. Dave had given Craig Sophia's father's number, but every time Craig called, there was no answer. Not even an answering machine. He arrived on Sunday and spent the first two days taking his parents out for lunch, tea, dinner, and a production of a contemporary musical. It was so boring, they left half way through. It seemed like he had been back for weeks. He tried again and finally got through.

"Hello? Is this Sophia Martin's residence?"

"Actually, it's mine, currently, but yes, it is Sophia's residence. Who's calling please?"

"Craig Matthews."

"I'm afraid she's not in," Sophia's father said kindly.

"Do you know how I can reach her?"

"She's not in London son."

"Oh…" Craig's mind was filling up with visions of Sophia lying on a beach in Ibiza or the Greek islands with a steamy Latin lover. "Do you know when she'll be back? And do you know if there is any way I can reach her?"

"Yes. Is it urgent?"

"Yes," Craig said like a little boy pleading with his kind elderly father.

"Alright son. Hold on a sec. I'll just go and get the number." Daniel got up from his favourite armchair, put his pipe down and looked for his phone book. Craig could hear him shuffling around in the background. "Here it is." Daniel picked up his pipe and resumed his 'after work' position. Every night he would come home from work, sit on his armchair and reflect upon his life. He used those moments for meditation. "The number is 2365 44577."

Craig wrote it down. "Wait that's an Asian city num…"

"Yes, that's a foreign number son, 852 before it."

"Did she move back there?" Craig asked with urgency in his voice.

"Don't think so."

"When will she back?" he asked, his urgency still lingering in the blue part of his chakra, trembling, shaking, and making his heart beat fast and furiously.

"Her brother has got himself into a fix again. Could be a few days, a week, or even a month?"

Craig felt like an idiot. Their paths kept crossing, not in a positive way, but in a completely negative one.

"Thank you Mr. Martin."

"Very welcome indeed. If she calls, I will let her know you rang."

"Cheers."

Both men put the phone down and Craig was very angry. He was not going to chase this girl he branded as 'silly' around. He was grateful he hadn't told his parents about this silly, silly girl… woman… girl… or whatever she was acting like right now. He had a very overcast image of her in his mind. One that was flighty and never grounded for long, always escaping. Never finding. Always seeking but never truly understanding that running was always a bad shift; one that never let you move forward.

Chapter 30

South East Asia

Sophia was standing in the middle of her old flat. Dave and Sophia had checked Alister into the Baptist Hospital because it was close to home. The doctor said he could have died. Alister was getting agitated and desperately wanted to go home.

Sophia entered first and was greeted by an overpowering aroma of bile, rotten food, piss and unwashed clothes. The stench shot up her nose. The air and sight were both revolting and sickening.

The kitchen had an overwhelming number of dirty dishes piled up in the sink. She picked some of them up and a nest of maggots seemed to hiss at her, their slimy pinkish white bodies crawling in a cesspool of muck. She let out a soft yelp as she released the dish. It missed its original place, hit the floor, and smashed into pieces.

Her bedroom was incredibly dusty and her white bed sheet was grey.

The living room hadn't been cleaned in months and Alister's clothes were scattered all over the place. She climbed over his clothes and slowly inched her way to her brother's room. The pungent smell of mouldy food particles, saliva, and urine greeted her, and unwashed clothes were strewn all over his room. She couldn't even open the door. She was afraid mice might even be living in the flat.

She crept into his room with disgust. She saw his guitar smashed in half and an overly dramatic smear of pathetic lyrics written on a big sheet of A3 paper. It was Alister's writing. The lyrics were insipid, silly and utterly childish.

I love you, let me go. You hurt me, I feel so low. Why did you do this, when everything we had was already burned in our kiss. I wanted a future with you. YOU WHORE!! YOU BITCH!!! YOU MEAN NOTHING TO ME!! I MEAN NOTHING TO YOU... *my needle... and I cry and I cry...*

It ended there.

Sophia was fuming. She wanted to kill Alister. She felt her face turn sour and her eyes squinted into very thin linear crevices, like a hawk searching for its prey.

She locked up the putrid flat and marched down to Baptist Hospital with the silly piece of paper in her hand. She barged into his room. They had taken the restraints off his arms, but left the ones on his legs. When he was withdrawing he was shaking so much they had to tie him down.

He was semi upright in bed and was channel surfing. "Hey Sophia." He said with a very disgruntled, bored and arrogant heir.

She was glaring at him. The hawk in her wanted to bite his head off. "Who the bloody hell do you think you are Alister Martin? Have you seen the state of Uncle Peter's flat?"

"IT'S YOUR FAULT!" He shouted.

"Listen you ungrateful boy! You have no idea what you have put me, Dad and Mum through. How dare do you think something as small as a *break up* constitutes your actions and your appalling behaviour? I am so disgusted at the fact that we have the same blood running through our veins. I have never met a more selfish person in my life."

"Don't be so dramatic Sophia." Alister turned away from her and turned up the volume on the TV. She was livid. She marched over to the bed, grabbed the remote control out of his hands and switched it off.

"Hey what are you doing you crazy cow!" he yelled.

Sophia was pointing the remote control at him like a gun. "I am going to make you listen to me if it's the last thing I ever do!" she said with her teeth gritted so hard that it felt like slate and dust were gurgling at the back of her throat, ready to spit out her very hurtful but truthful words.

"You... don't... understand." Alister scowled like a little boy.

Sophia walked stealthily closer to him, with the remote control poised towards the centre of his neck, as if to shove it down his throat, her eyes like hawks and her teeth shut tightly in her mouth; Alister could see the balls on the sides of her jaw line pulsating with venom, fear, anger, and disappointment. As she spoke she spat out her words with utter frustration. It emerged as her soul's bedrock of absolute sadness.

"What don't I understand? All I can see is a waste of a human being sitting in front of me! If you want to kill yourself Alister then go ahead, but don't involve the family anymore! I have had enough. Look at you. Look at what you have become. You constantly keep regressing and this is the last time you are going to do this to me or anyone!! I have had enough!!! Whenever I think you have grown up and become mature, you prove Mum, Dad and me wrong!! I don't care if you have to stay in the hospital for the rest of your life, because your abuse is wearing us down. No one in the world is going to help you unless you help yourself. Do you understand?!! Do you!!!?"

Alister wasn't responding; he was staring at the wall in front of him. He wanted to go home immediately and take care of the pain through drastic measures. He knew he was completely alone in the world.

"Why aren't you responding? Do you want me to beg you, again, to talk to me? Well, you listen here!! I am not going to pander to you and your idiotic ways. If you can't value your own life, then I can't be bothered to value it for you!" She threw the remote control on the side table. "And this stupid, stupid poem you wrote over a stupid, stupid, stupid girl is pitiable. You need to grow up. And fast. I have had enough of facilitating to your disgusting depressions, which make no sense!" She crumpled the piece of paper into a small ball; threw it on his bed, near his face, and left the room.

Alister felt nothing but frustration. He wanted to chew off the restraints and his ankles and run away forever. He wanted to go back to his heroin filled days, where no one could find him, and where colours of a different day would assist in his decline. He began to shake and punch the side of the bed in a repetitive action, his punching getting stronger and stronger with each molecule in his body consumed by frustration, anger and a lack of decision making. The nurse came in swiftly and injected him with another dose of Valium. His body suddenly began to relax and his frustration slowly calmed into silent sobs, lost in a drift of some unrealistic fantasy dream-land of sleep.

Sophia walked out of the hospital and literally felt like she had nowhere to go. She didn't want to go back to her old flat, and she didn't feel like calling Dave. She walked for ten minutes to Festival Walk and sat down to have a coffee. She wasn't crying. She felt a sense of relief, like she had sprouted wings. She knew telling her brother the truth was going to help her get him on the next flight back to London as soon as possible. First, she was going to clean up the flat, and try to get her brother to come back with her so he could be taken care of at a rehabilitation hospital in Surrey where he could be close to his family.

Her father was absolutely right. Alister needed some kind of foundation as well as change.

Chapter 31

London

Mala and Sharon were discussing marriage at Bazica. They had already consumed two cappuccinos each. They were giggling at the prospect of what Mala's mother would do when or *if* she ever found out about Washington. Sharon always accused Mala of being a tad bit racist when she referred to Washington as 'black.' It was always a philosophical question, because the little fiery red head with emerald green eyes was incredible at never putting 'colour' labels on people. She would often wonder if Mala thought of herself as 'brown' or Noor as 'beige.'

Sharon interjected, "Don't fret too much. Maybe you are unsure of marriage… so you are creating a sub plot… based around 'colour,' to actually deflect the fact that you are scared to marry Washington, because of what your mother will think, and because you are so old already."

"Come on Sharon," Mala retorted. "I really do love him. I *am* getting old, and I know that culture cannot be my impetus for decision making and shifts in my life."

"Then stop struggling Mala. I've got a doctor's appointment," Sharon said sipping on her last drop of foam at the bottom of her coffee cup.

"Do you need me to go with you? Are you okay?" Mala asked with concern.

It's a routine check-up, nothing to worry about," Sharon said, sneakily taking a cigarette out of her pocket. She waved her hands in the air to signal to Fatima. "Please put these on my tab doll."

"Fatima looks like she has gained a little bit of weight. Do you think she is pregnant?" asked Mala as she stared at Fatima walking away from their table. It looked like her hips had grown. Mala felt like a real aunty, talking about the young generation.

Fatima came over to the table for Sharon to sign the tab. "How's it going hun?" Sharon asked as smoke swirled above her head.

"Good, good. I have actually started night school. My father is allowing me to go."

"That is so wonderful." Mala said retracting her thoughts about Fatima being pregnant. The rumours in her own mind could be so wrong and judgmental sometimes. "So when are you getting married, like your father wants, if you are going to school at night?"

Fatima leaned closer to the two women, and said. "Soon... I am getting married soon. Very soon. It's a secret, my father doesn't know yet."

Sharon and Mala looked at each other, stunned.

"Why haven't you told your father Fatima?" Mala inquired like the truest version of her older self, which was indeed an Indian *aunty*.

"He's not Lebanese," she said putting her index finger to her lips, her grey eyes piercing into Mala's dark brown eyes, which looked like seas of dark almond syrup.

"This is getting spicy," Sharon said as she leaned even closer into the table. More smoke was percolating over her head. "Where is he from?"

"He's from here, he is English."

"Wow," Mala said ironically as she sat back in her chair. She wondered what Fatima's father would say if her boyfriend was 'black.' Or a 'black' Lebanese, would that matter? Why was keeping to heritage and DNA so important for ancient civilisations? She knew her mother would never approve of Washington. She could feel

Fatima's dilemma. Even her generation were subjected to the ancient paradigms. How was one to shift? It always had to be a revolutionary. Mala knew she was old, how could she be a revolutionary? Maybe it would be Fatima. "I'm so happy for you Fatima."

"Please don't tell my father," she said as he shouted from behind the counter for his daughter to prepare six cappuccinos and six breakfast croissants for the six business men sitting at a very low frequency table.

Both friends parted and Mala made her way back to her flat. She was going to try and call her mother again. Washington was home when she got there and looked like he had a lot on his mind.

"Hey lover, what are you doing?" she said as she walked in the door.

Washington was looking under a cabinet in the living room. His instruments would sometimes get under those cabinets, or pieces of paper he had written on. "I am trying to look for a piece of music I wrote about six months ago. I put it in this book I was reading and now I can't find it."

"What is the name of the book?" Mala asked as she stared at his beautiful strong body. "Have you tried to look on the book shelf in the study?"

"Yeah twice already. I can't find it. It's called the *Path of Masters*. It's a big red book."

"Maybe you left it in Cannes."

"Maybe." Washington sighed as he got up off his knees. He was tired of looking.

"Are you busy tonight Washington?"

"Yeah baby, I have to work."

"I need to talk to you about something urgent."

"Can it wait Mala? I have to get organised for tonight." He sounded frustrated.

Mala knew it wasn't the right time to mention her plans for moving.

"Someone called for you today," he said in a sombre tone.

"Who?" Mala asked with a tinge of urgency.

"Some lady."

"My mother?"

"Yeh, could be… but I asked her if she was your mother and she said no."

"Did she ask who you were?"

"Not really," Washington was getting his instruments ready, he wasn't paying much attention to Mala.

"Washington, stop… for a second… please. I want to know the whole conversation please."

"She asked if you were in. I said no. She asked, 'who is this?' And I replied Washington, and I asked her who she was and she told me her name was Durga. And then I asked her if she was your mother and she replied, 'no.' And then she asked who I was and I told her I was your boyfriend. She was silent and then asked for you to call her back." He resumed packing his bag of instruments.

"What time did she call?"

"A few hours ago."

"Were you sleeping when she called? Did you sound like you had just woken up?"

"Of course Mala, she woke me up from my sleep. What's the big deal? What's the matter, why do you look like that? She doesn't know about… us… does she?"

Mala was silent.

"Are you going to tell her?"

Mala didn't know what to say.

"Am I going to remain a phantom boyfriend?" Washington was not happy.

And then Mala said the unthinkable… or maybe an impulsive response. "Not until you marry me."

"Okay so let's do it Mala. Right now… right here… will you marry me?"

"Don't ask me like that Washington. It has to be real. I don't want to play silly games. And I can't take you seriously when you are acting like it's no big deal."

"Who's playing games here Mala? I am asking you a serious question… like I said… will you marry me?"

"I hate games Washington, I really do." She harrumphed into the kitchen.

"Really?" he asked with sarcasm as he followed her into the kitchen.

"Yes. *Really…*" she said imitating him.

"The game ends, Mala when you decide. Not me." He picked up his bags, left the house and slammed the door behind him.

Five minutes later the doorbell rang.

"You have your keys Washington. Open the door by yourself." There was no answer. Mala was still standing in the kitchen with her back to the door. The doorbell rang again. She glared at the door with all her might and scolded the peep hole while envisioning her *boyfriend's* face. "Washington, I'm not playing anymore. Use. Your. Key." There was still no response. She walked out of the kitchen and stood in front of the door with her arms folded. The doorbell kept ringing. She was scowling now, and as soon as she opened the door, prepared a round of ammunition of words to shoot at Washington.

"Think you are funny right? Well… the door was wide open." She stopped in her tracks and realised it wasn't Washington. "Oh, hello." It was Mr. Sticks, the young lawyer.

"This is for you Ms. Amani. Sorry to intrude again." He handed an envelope to her. "Inside, you will find the total sum of the inheritance; as per your father's will, we have divided it equally between you and your sister. If there are any problems, or if you have any queries, please contact us. Once again, my apologies for barging in on you." He smirked as he made his way to leave. First the knife incident and now her shouting at Washington about the keys; Sticks must have thought Mala was a lunatic.

She opened the envelope and inside was a check as well as a document for a property in California. It was her old address. When she looked at the numbers on the check, she couldn't believe her eyes. She was astonished.

She called her sister.

"Mila, did you get the papers? Did you see how much money we got?"

"How much did you get?" Her younger sister inquired, wondering if she would be short changed because of the age difference.

"Two hundred and fifty thousand US dollars."

"Me too," Mila replied feeling guilty for not trusting that her father would look after her in the same way as her older sibling. "What are we going to do with all this money?"

"Save it of course, my sweet young sister. Open up a separate bank account, just in your name, nobody else's. Don't tell anyone Mila. Not even Maneck okay? Have you spoken to him about going to go see Mama in Bombay for a few weeks?"

"No I haven't," Mila sighed. "Have you told Washington yet?"

"I tried but it just got complicated because he was about to go to work and we didn't have time to communicate. It was just words and threats about marriage. Nothing whatsoever to do with love, celebration or liberation," Mala said as she recalled the conversation with Washington. She felt embarrassed.

Mila interrupted her older sister's thoughts. "I'm a bit scared Mala, to leave England... it seems so backward in India..."

"I know... but don't worry... we both know that we need to be amongst family and we found our mother again, so it would be wise to seek her out again. Give her a second chance."

"So, what property did he leave in your name Mila?"

There was a bit of an uncomfortable silence. "Our place in Delhi." Mila replied.

"I know that house well, I was born there."

"So why didn't he leave it to you?" Mila asked with confusion.

"Because he thought I became too *American*." Mala sighed.

"Why are you sighing Mala? Is the house really ugly?"

"No, not at all. It's huge. With a stunning terrace and a garden. It probably needs a little bit of renovation. It's a really classy house, very colonial. It's 'Oxford House' right?"

"Yes it is," Mila said looking at the property bond in her name. "Did you get Parkfields Drive?"

"Yeah." Mala sighed again. "So many bad memories there. I don't think I ever want to go back and live in California. Those days were so harsh. I think I'm going to rent it out and make money out of a sad property situation."

Mala and Mila talked about their childhood for two hours. At first, there was a melancholic tone in their voices but after evoking humorous aspects of their lives, they began to feel more relaxed.

"Do you remember that big ostentatious wooden backgammon table we had in the den? The one with cookie sized marble chips?" Mila recalled.

"Yes, I remember, we used to play *market market* and we would pretend the white chips were fish and the brown ones were beef. And when Papa found out he got so mad, he hid all the marble chips like they were bars of gold."

Both girls were giggling. "And do you remember what we did after he confiscated them from us? We went into the pantry cupboard downstairs where Mama kept all the extra toiletries like shampoo, soap, tooth brushes, and toilet paper, and we played *supermarket supermarket* instead." Mala was laughing.

"Do you remember mama's face when she found out that we had used all of her 'emergency supplies' for our games?" Mila was smiling.

"We had so much fun when we were growing up. We had a really good childhood, when we were together away from our parent's incessant fighting."

"I can't wait to see Mama and remind her of the good times we used to have."

"Me too," Mala said, with stubbornness slowly melting away from her.

After another hour on the phone. Mila had to go look after her youngest. She felt at peace with herself, and was still laughing at herself for all the silly, mischievous and interesting incidents she and her sister used to get up to in their childhood. She felt blessed to have such a strong, intelligent and heartwarming sister.

Mala got off the phone with her sister and smiled at the *market market* story. She adored her little sister for all her strength, beauty and compassion. She was left thinking of how to tell Washington. Her stomach began to hurt again. She wanted her family and Washington at the same time. It was up to her to make a difference as well as change.

Chapter 32

London

Sharon was lying in a hospital bed. Her routine check-up had turned out to be bad news. The doctors had warned her several times about the implications and complications that smoking would have on her body. She never took heed.

Mala was alarmed when Sandy broke the news to her – a biopsy concerning a lump inside her daughter's throat was making her panic. Mala told her not to worry and promised Ms. Connell she would come by to the hospital in the afternoon. Sandy was pottering around her daughter's bed, making sure she was comfortable.

"Please don't agonize over this mum."

"I'm not worried doll." Sharon knew her mother was lying through her teeth. "I know everything will be fine. Do you need anything doll?" Sandy placed her hand on Sharon's forehead. "I think you have a temperature."

"Come on now Mum, stop making all this fuss."

Sandy sat down by her daughter's bedside. She didn't want to start crying. She checked the time on her watch, it was almost half past four. Mala would be there soon. Sharon took a short nap. She didn't feel the slightest bit worried. 'Just another test, to see how far Sharon Connell can be pushed,' she thought to herself.

Mala showed up at the hospital around 5:30 p.m. She bought Sandy a huge bouquet of flowers and a packet of Nicorette chewing gum for Sharon. It was wrapped in hideous wrapping paper embellished with the 'no entry' sign. Atop the present was a huge bow. It was the most sarcastic present Sharon had ever received.

Mala hugged Sharon and Sandy tightly. Sandy looked at Mala up and down and gave her another hug, squeezing her even tighter this time.

"Golly Mala, look at you, you beautiful lass. You're glowing."

"I stopped smoking Ms. Connell, and I'm doing yoga now."

"You should give your friend over here some advice, and a good lecture," Sandy said, shifting her eyes over to her daughter.

"No lecture from either of you," Sharon said looking at her best friend and her mother from side to side like a tennis match.

"What time is the biopsy? And what did the doctor say?" Mala inquired.

"Biopsy in the morning and then we get the results in the evening. That's when he will tell me if the cells in my throat are cancerous or… if they're not. Bloody hell, I have to wake up so early tomorrow."

"How did this happen?" Mala wasn't feeling so chirpy anymore. On the contrary, she was feeling quite worried and disillusioned.

I went for a routine check-up and the doctor noticed my cough hadn't subsided. She took a swab, and as they say… the rest is history."

"Sharon… I'm so sorry."

"About what?"

"All this."

Mala looked over at Sandy; she was beside herself with grief.

After the hospital Mala felt ill. She prayed for Sharon on her way to yoga. 'Please angels, take care of my best friend. Make her well and make sure she is safe from harm. Keep Sandy happy and please don't let anything terrible happen to our beautiful girl.'

She stepped into the yoga studio and very pleasant looking gentleman approached her.

"Hi Mala. You don't recognize me do you?" The man was handsome and tall. He had mousy blonde hair and a goatee.

"Jeremy?"

"Yeah."

"Hey, how are you? Gosh I haven't seen you in ages. How have you been?"

"I've been really well Mala, I have been out of London for a while now. I am actually doing business abroad in Germany."

"Wow, that's wonderful." Mala couldn't believe she was talking to him. "Are you back for good now?"

"We'll see. I'm getting married in a fortnight and my fiancée is based here."

"Congratulations Jeremy. I am so happy for you." He had become so refined.

"Are you still teaching?" He remembered.

"Yes, and still loving it."

"How are Sharon and Annabelle?"

"Actually, Sharon is in the hospital."

"Sorry to hear that. Please give her my regards. And Annabelle?"

"To tell you the truth Jeremy…"

"You haven't heard from her…"

"In a long time," Mala said with hurt.

"Typical Annabelle," he said with irony.

"She seemed happy the last time I saw her."

"Then I am happy for her," he said graciously.

Master Kamal interrupted everybody. "*Class ve are going to begin now. Please find a space and start your jourrrrney tovords your centerrrr.*" Everyone stopped and like robotic yogis found a space. Jeremy whispered to Mala. "If you do see her again soon, send her a warm hello from me." Mala smiled at him as everyone in class chanted "*auuuuummmmmm.*"

Chapter 33

South East Asia

Alister was still in hospital. The doctor recommended he stay longer because of his condition. They were afraid he would relapse and end up dead.

Sophia saw Dave once whilst she was there. Not because she didn't want to, but because both of them were so busy. Dave was spending more time with Sergio. And Sophia was restoring her old flat.

"It took me seven days to complete everything. I don't envy God. Just one flat and I'm exhausted." Both Dave and Sophia were sipping on their cappuccinos in Central. It was Sunday evening and the streets were rather empty.

"Are you alright petal?"

"I'm good, I have decided to take Alister back with me. He made a huge fuss about his band and Hong Kong being his home. So I got Lionel, Kay, Darius and Clive to come to hospital and tell him he was out of the band."

"Crickey! How did he take that?" Dave asked with his eyes brimming over his cappuccino foam.

"Very badly… I mean, this is the best thing for him. How can he stay here alone? He has no responsibility. And I definitely don't want to move back here. Because I try so hard to walk down this straight road and when there is a curve, in this metaphoric road, I don't embrace it. I run away from it and it leaves me wondering, pondering, stressing and…"

Dave interrupted. "Alone?"

"No. Lonely."

"Oh petal…" Dave grabbed her delicate Asian hands. He didn't know what else to say.

She put her other hand on his hands and said, "You were absolutely right when you said what you said on New Year's Day. That *if God brings you to it he will bring you through it.*"

"So, do you believe me now?"

"Yes I do Dave," she said staring down at his wrinkly hands. "Maybe you helped me manifest something I didn't want to happen."

Dave chuckled. "I'm not God Sophia, unless of course, you want me to be… I don't mind the attention."

"So, tell me about Sergio."

"I'm in love, lust, and everything nice."

They spoke more about Sergio, and Dave couldn't help getting into the personal and physical details of the relationship. At these points in the conversation, Sophia put her hands over her ears and sang. These moments gave her glimpses into Craig and his adorable ways.

Chapter 34

London

That night, Mala changed her life forever.

"What do you mean you are going to live with your mother for some time? Why can't she come here and why did you wait so long to tell me?" Washington was agitated.

"It's far for her to travel, and she has a husband, a home and everything set up there. I didn't want to tell you because of the way you would react."

"Well, I'm not excited if that's what you wanted to see. And we had plans…"

"What plans Washington? Tell me what plans," her tone was getting edgier.

"Plans to get married Mala…"

"What? You have never asked me sincerely. I want my mother to accept us." She had deep confusion swirling around in her. Her green light, yellow light was dull… dim… unclear.

"Your mother who you haven't seen in how many years? Ummm… let me see… 20 something… years… I see. You want someone who doesn't know you… to accept you…" He started to laugh a very sarcastic laugh. "You are going to change Mala? Or change the world and make people accept me? You Indians can't even realise for one second that you are but only one… one shade lighter than an African man... you walk around London thinking you are white... your culture is racist..."

"That's unfair." Mala pleaded. "I don't want to have hang ups about race, culture or nationality like our parents and grandparents did. I want to live in a world where people are colour blind. Their understanding of culture and their old paradigms will not make us go forward Washington... please listen to me..."

He interrupted harshly, pacing like a panther. "Spare me Mala. For centuries, people have fought because of race, culture, ideologies, politics and whatever... watch the news, you will see it every day..."

"I know it's out there, but it just takes one person to make a shift, to help with the domino effect. Make people feel the changes in them and embrace them through love."

"Then you have a lot to learn!" He was angrier than ever before.

"So, this is going to turn into an argument rather than a discussion is it? Are you going to sit there and attack me, because of the way I perceive life? You should know me better than that. And if we can't see eye to eye on something fundamental in our lives, like marriage, then I don't see what the point is of us staying together then. Loving each other is also about understanding each other."

Washington's laugh was piercingly sarcastic and forced. "You are a contradiction Mala. First, you say that race and colour don't mean anything and then you talk about your mother's acceptance and then you talk about marriage. Make up your mind, where is this conversation going? You sound muddled."

"I don't want to argue with you. I love you Washington. I've been with you for eighteen years now. Not because I have to, but because I choose to. And you have brought so much inspiration into my life. I can't begin to tell you..."

Washington sat down and rubbed his head with the top of his palm like an old Indian *uncle*. "Okay, okay... I'm sorry... I don't want to fight either..."

Mala sat next to him. "Don't apologise for anything. We are individuals, we all have the right to an opinion. I just want us to be on the same page, the same team, the same everything…"

"So what do you want me to do?" he asked looking at her.

"I can't tell you what to do. I don't want to tell you what to do. I want you to do what makes you happy. But I am telling you my plans, not because I am being selfish or giving you an ultimatum or pressuring you to do anything okay? But I have to leave for a while and go and see my mother." Mala leaned across the sofa and tenderly placed a kiss on his big lips. She was strong today and she wanted Washington to understand her. Deeply, in a way which made them see life like adults. He kissed her back and put his head on her chest.

"I don't want to lose you princess. What if she can't accept us? Our love and connection is old, ancient and real. I can't marry you right now, because I don't have enough money."

Mala knew why she fell in love with him. He was both passionate and tender. She leaned in closer to him. "Washington, listen to me. So much of what we go through in life is so unpredictable. We can't keep on waiting for something to happen; if we don't make things happen for ourselves we will never move forward. Using money as an obstacle only makes the situation worse. It is putting blame on a circumstance we are creating. We have to make things work for us."

"I love you so much Mala."

"I love you too Washington, so much."

"But… I really have to tell you, that I am not ready for marriage. It is in my culture to be the provider and I feel ashamed that I can't be the sole provider."

"I understand." Mala truly understood how culture got in the way.

"And I never want you to leave me, because of this ancient way of thinking. I don't know how to change it. It's just inbred, stuck…"

"I'm not dying Washington. I'll be back in two or three months. And I'm not leaving for another three, so don't fret. Everything will work out just the way we want it when the time is right."

He looked up at her again, and he looked like he had been tearing up. His eyes were red. "I will ask for your hand in marriage before you go. I promise. From now until then, I am going to work harder and save more money so we can have a life together one day."

"Don't make promises you can't keep Washington. I have been through so many fragile moments this past year. I don't feel like being let down again. I understand that you are not ready but I want you to know that I need to regroup with my family. I hope one day we can all accept each other as one family. I can't change what you are feeling, and like I said, I am not put on this earth to pressure you..."

"Please give me some time Mala."

"I will, you have all the time from me Washington. I am leaving in three months, and I hope I am no longer than two months in Asia, but just know, and I mean this from the bottom of my heart... even if there is no proposal... I will always love you."

Washington hugged his woman tightly and began to cry on her shoulder. He wanted his princess to be with him for the rest of his life, but he was feeling tremendously insecure about her family and her wealth. He wanted the world's acceptance, but he realised he couldn't obtain this feeling until he made peace with his own issues. All he wanted was to be a provider, a strong man for his woman and not a failure like his father. Washington's mother had left his father when Washington was sixteen, because he couldn't provide for her or the family. He spent all their money on alcohol and by the time Washington turned eighteen, his father had already drunk himself to death.

He couldn't seem to get over the notion that Mala was willing to work as a team and help him. His culture had always taught him the 'man' was the provider.

Maybe Mala was right, it was time for his generation to make a difference, to show generations before that life does evolve and values change.

Despite these ideas, Washington had to understand and grasp that love was the only thing that remained a constant, since the beginning of time. And with an abundance of love in one's heart, life became the easiest wave to ride.

The next morning Mala woke up with no fear in her heart and a vision towards her own future. She knew what she wanted and it was all up to her now. Nothing or no one could make her feel like life was difficult. Her father always talked about karma and she remembered him speaking to her about that concept often. He reminded her that we all come into this world alone and we leave with a robe of karma… *"So, Malsy, alvays be a good girl Beti… Karma is real."* This morning, her father's voice was bouncing around the windows of her mind.

Her students brought new meaning to her life and she saw them as little souls reflecting the future of existence. They were indeed more intelligent than she was at their age. After school, she still hadn't heard from Sharon or Sandy, so she took it upon herself to take the train down to Surrey to visit her best friend.

When she walked into the hospital room, Mala's brown face turned into a dusky hue which made her look twenty years or more older. Her best friend was laying there with no expression on her face. A massive bandage around her neck and a puffy protruding piece of gauze splattered with a dash of puss and blood was splayed right across her throat. Sandy was holding her daughter's hand with a large amount of tears streaming heavily down her face like a hurricane of sadness with no sound. Both of them were still, as if in a tableau.

Sharon tried to speak, but nothing came out accept a murmur of wind. Her mother stood up and wailed on Mala's shoulder, giving credence and sound to her over flowing tears and sadness. "She's going to die Mala… my precious baby… is going to die… I can't believe it… I wasn't answered… my prayers were all in vain… the doctor says she has cancer. But she can't. She is young… not like me lass… look at her… my precious… Mala help me…" She was out of control.

Mala peeled Sandy off her shoulder and helped her sit down.

She knelt down by the chair and whispered. "Listen, now get a hold of yourself. We are going to get through this. Don't worry. All this crying is not going to help Sharon at all... on the contrary, she will be more stressed if she sees any of us like this. Okay? Be strong okay." Mala was rubbing Sandy's shoulders. She knew the poor woman needed more than comforting. She handed her the box of tissues. And Mala walked closer to her best friend's bedside.

Sharon stirred and tried to say something, but a whistling sound came out from under the bandage. She managed a weak smile and Mala motioned for her to keep still.

"We are here for you Sharon, don't worry about anything. Everything is going to be fine. You hear me Sharon?"

Sharon tried to nod, and Mala could see a faded flicker in her eye.

"I am going to take your mother down to the canteen for some coffee okay? We will be back shortly. Don't go anywhere my gorgeous *aunty*," Mala said as she was trying to find some kind of humour in this dire situation. She knew she had to be strong for the Connells.

Sharon looked over to the side table and Mala followed her gaze, she could see that her friend wanted pen and paper. She handed her the hospital stationary and a pencil. She tried to write but she was still weak from the drugs and her handwriting looked like chicken scratches. She wrote:

Thank you Mala. I love you.

Mala looked at the piece of paper and kissed her friend on the forehead. "I love you too. Now you get some rest and we will be back soon."

Sharon closed her eyes and rested while Mala took Sandy for a coffee.

In the canteen, Mala urged Ms. Connell to calm down and asked for the details of the biopsy.

"They said she would be fine. My baby is going to die Mala. Is she? Do you think she will?" Sandy began to sob again.

"Ms. Connell, please don't say that. You must be strong for Sharon right now. We can't instil fear into her, because if we do, then she may never recover." Mala was rubbing Sandy's shoulders again. She was trying her best to comfort her.

"Yes, I know what you are saying lass. I have to be the pillar. I know..."

"So what did the doctor say about the biopsy?"

"They said... the lump in her throat was malignant, and they wanted to remove it and then do chemotherapy. And they want to start the treatment as soon as possible. And I wanted to ask for a second opinion, but she looks like she is in so much pain. Maybe when she is stronger later on today or tomorrow we can discuss with her..."

"No!" Mala interrupted. "She is going to say she wants to leave... and you know how stubborn she is. So it is up to me and you to convince her to stay for a little while longer."

"Will you help me Mala?"

"Of course I will. But first, I want you to go home, have a shower, wash the day off, put on some fresh clothes and come back later."

"What about Sharon?"

"I will be with her, don't worry. I am here for her. As well as you. I will be here while you're gone."

"Are you sure?" Sandy lit up very slightly. The poor lady needed a break.

"She is my best friend Ms. Connell. Don't worry about it. I promise you I will be here when you get back. And when you come back, I want you to shine for Sharon. Remember that faith and confidence will help her get through this."

"Thank you Mala, thank you. You are a wonderful lass."

"I will see you later," Mala said as she kissed Sandy on the cheek. They walked down to the lobby and Mala saw her off. The hospital was the best in the country and had the finest doctors from all over the world working there. She called the valet and he brought Sandy's car around. She drove off and Mala walked back into room 332.

An unbelievable sadness loomed over her as the thought of Sharon being absent from her life haunted her. She couldn't imagine life without her. As she slowly walked back to the room, the smell of antiseptic made her shudder. The white walls looked like a transition room between heaven and hell. All she could think about was Sharon lying in a bed unable to speak. 'What the hell is going on?' she was screaming in her head.

Chapter 35

London

Washington was at home when Mala got there. She was so drowsy. She felt like she could sleep for days.

"What's up princess?"

"Sharon is in hospital."

"What!"

"Ya. Throat cancer."

"Jesus Christ baby."

"I know."

"Is she going to be fine?"

"Hope so."

Washington ran Mala a bath and prepared a bowl of hot soup for her. She looked rough today. When she finished her meal, he tucked her into bed and watched football in the living room.

Sophia and Alister arrived at Heathrow, and Daniel was there to greet his children. Alister didn't say anything during the flight back to London and Sophia didn't mind one bit.

"Hi Alister… son," Daniel reached out for his son, but Alister made no effort to greet his father properly.

"Hi Dad."

"Hi Sophia. Are you alright?" Daniel asked as he hugged his daughter tightly.

"Exhausted to say the least Dad." She hugged him back generously.

"Did you tell Alister what we have decided?" Daniel was speaking as if Alister was in a different room. He continued to push his son's wheelchair towards the carpark. Alister had lost so much weight in the past weeks, his frail body couldn't handle any kind of physical endurance, not even walking.

"What have you decided for me? I don't want to be here! I can't stand any of you. I wish I was dead, or you were dead. This is the worst family in the world. All you have ever done is trap me." Alister looked like a livid zombie-esque creature, spitting out negative ammunition from his mouth. Words he never thought before came out of his horrid mouth.

Sophia ignored him. "He has no choice Dad, we are taking him to the hospital."

"PISS OFF SOPHIA! I can make my own decisions, and as soon as I'm better, I'm leaving. You can't check me into hospital without my permission or consent. I am a grown man."

"Alister, shut up please. I am trying to have a mature conversation with our father."

"You bitch! Just like Mum!"

Daniel halted the wheelchair in a very rough manner and glared at his son. "Now you listen here boy, you have some growing up to do, and if it means you have to stay in hospital for years, until you get your bloody act together, then so be it. And don't you ever, ever, speak to your sister like that again. You selfish, ungrateful boy," Daniel was firm and remained calm, as he spoke.

Sophia had spoken to Dr. Sum at the Baptist Hospital about Alister, who had refused to seek treatment at a hospital near their home in Surrey. Dr. Sum later wrote a letter instructing the Critical Care Unit for Rehabilitation in charge of Alister's case that he was in a life threatening situation. Sophia signed the form with great relief and knew that this meant no turning back for Alister.

The Martin family drove to the hospital in silence.

Craig was back in Hong Kong. He had left Heathrow, once again, with confidence and the promise of new adventures. He arrived back into Happy Valley with a new outlook, which made him feel fresh and alive. He was going to tackle the Asian city, one more time. Subtracting Jennifer, Sophia, Dave, and even his long-time friend Tomas, he was fully charged for a new chapter in his life.

Annabelle Noor was getting fatter and fatter by the minute while Ahmed was getting increasingly more tyrannical. Maybe she liked the rough kind, but it was doing her no justice whatsoever.

The phone rang at eleven thirty at night. Mala was fast asleep when Washington woke her up.

"Mala, baby… Maaaalaaaaa… babe… wake up."

"No Washington, please, I'm so tired."

"I think it's your mother on the phone."

Mala shot up like a bolt of lightning and took the phone from Washington.

"Hello?"

"*Mala?*"

"Mama?"

"*Ey Beti, how are you?*" She still spoke the same way, with an Indian accent and a soft tone.

"Mama I have been trying to call you for so long."

"*I know, I know... Mila told me.*"

"How are you?" Mala sat upright and turned on the bedside table lamp.

"*I'm fine vot about you?*"

"I'm good, what are you doing in India?"

"*I got married.*" Durga was smiling while talking. She sounded happy.

"I am so pleased for you Mama, is he a good guy?"

"*Haaaa haaaaa... he is very sveet.*"

"Does he look after you?"

"*Yes. He really does... What about you? Who is that man that picked up the phone?*"

"Umm... Umm... Ahh..." Mala was stalling as well as hesitating.

"*Boy friend?*"

"Yes."

"*Hai haaaa. Living together?*"

"Yes."

"*Vhy?*"

"We love each other."

"*You don't sound sure Beti, vot is vrong. Is he good to you? He doesn't hurt you does he?*"

"No Mama. No... not at all... nothing like that. I was worried about you."

"*Vot… me liking the idea?*"

"Yes."

"*Vell… I don't.*"

"Mama, you haven't been in my life for so long; how can you say that?"

"*I can. I am your mother. And alvays vill be.*"

"So, where were you when Mila and I were growing up?" Mala didn't want the conversation to go pear shaped. She wanted to keep it calm and civil. A dark trap door seemed to bang shut in her mind, making her feel uneasy and suffocated. She wished she hadn't said that.

"*That is not fair Beti, you saw how your father treated me.*"

"And we told you to leave him."

"*I couldn't leave because of you and Mila.*"

"Mama, I don't want to talk about this now."

"*Then vhen do you vant to talk about it?*"

"Did Mila tell you our plan?"

"*Haa… Haaaa. How long vill you come for?*"

"I don't know, a few months."

"*You don't vant to live here?*"

"Mama, I don't want to live in India."

"*Are you bringing your boyfriend vith you?*"

"No, he has to work."

"*Vot does he do?*"

"He is a musician."

"*I see, and vhere is he from?*"

"The Caribbean."

"*Is he KHARO?!*"

"I hate that word Mama, please don't say that word in front of me."

"*Is he?*"

"What?"

"*Black.*"

"Yes, so what."

"*Oh my God! Please Shiva help you... My God!*"

"And where is your husband from?"

"*Amrika.*"

"Really?"

"*Ya.*"

"Should God be helping you too?"

"*Nee neee. Amrikan is okay. But black? KHARO? My God I don't know vot to say.*"

"Don't say anything Mama." But what Mala really wanted to say was more scathing: 'Well let me tell you something Mother. Washington has been more a part of my life than you have in God knows how long. If there is someone you should be praying for, it is yourself. What kind of mother do you call yourself? You think Santosh was bad, well you are worse. You were alive and you didn't even care to contact me or my sister. And then you send us this silly letter telling us you have risen and all this crap. I can't believe you have the nerve to lecture me about my life. You have no right! I am horrified to think that you will not accept me with open arms. If I was a beggar on the street would you treat me differently? Would you? You probably would just walk away and have no shame.'

But how could she even dream of saying that to the woman who gave birth to her? Durga was her mother and of course she would be concerned. Mala wanted peace. She loved her mother unconditionally and nothing was going to stop her from feeling and respecting that bond.

Not even her mother's preconceived notions of Washington.

"I can't wait to see you Mama."

"Me too Beti. Come sooner if you can. I hawe a surprise for you and Mila vhen you get here."

"Is it a baby?"

"EEEEE... eeeee Shiva God help you... I am so old ya... Are you kidding? No VAY! You vill see ven you two angels get here."

"Do you have an email address ma?"

"Haaa haaaa, but I never use it. It is too complicated for me."

"I will call you again soon Mama."

"I vill see you wery soon Beti. Ve hawe so much catching up to do, and I can't begin to tell you how sorry I am."

"Don't worry Ma. We have each other now." Mala was getting teary eyed. She couldn't wait to see her mother; she was going to talk to Mila about leaving a bit earlier.

When she put the phone down she felt more awake. She went outside into the living room. Washington was playing music. It sounded heavenly, like clouds singing in a harmonious orchestra filled with exotic melodies from all over the world.

"She called baby, she actually called." Mala was so happy.

"I know baby."

"She is so excited to see me."

"I am happy for you sweetheart." He stopped playing and looked at her. "Are you really leaving me babe?"

She paused and looked at the floor. "Not for good Washington... a few months... I promise."

Chapter 36

Surrey

Sharon was still in the same bed, and beside her was a boy who had checked in a week ago but new to her ward. Since he got there, he hadn't said one word to her or any one of his family, who visited him every day. Sharon was grateful for Mala and her mother visiting her all the time, because she really needed to speak.

"How are you feeling today Sharon?"

"Bloody good Mala," she said with some minor conviction in her voice. "I don't feel like I'm swallowing sand paper anymore."

"You look so much better Sharon," Mala said leaning in to kiss her best friend on the forehead again.

"I feel so much better," Sharon said with a smile.

"Okay... so here's a run-down of a few things. Let me do all the talking first and then you can reply. Just respond with a nod and not a wheeze... I called Mui Mui like you asked me to, and her mother says she will bring her to see you soon."

Sharon interrupted, "The bloody cow is lying, she wouldn't be caught dead around town with her own child."

Mala continued, ignoring this outbreak. "I also spoke to Neil, he says take as much time as you need. They've already found a substitu..."

She interrupted... again, "Bloody hell, it's only been ten days. Will you please reassure him that I will be back as soon as I'm better?"

"Sure, Sharon, I'll tell him, but don't worry. Your health is more important, and everyone at work understands. Washington is coming by later with Alex before work."

"Oh bless," Sharon sighed.

"Annabelle, do you want me to call her to let her know…"

"No! Absolutely not!"

"Oh and by the way, I met Jeremy at yoga the other day. He looks fantastic and has so much energy. He's getting married and has been working in Germany the whole time."

"Wow," was the only thing Sharon managed to say.

"So Noor missed out…" Mala said as she turned away from Sharon's bed to pour herself a glass of water.

"I don't want her to know I am in the hospital Mala. She has not been a part of my life for so long, her gossip and stories from afar are going to make me more depressed, and I definitely don't want this in her stupid book. Or as her *Ree. Search.*"

"No worries Sharon. Don't get riled up. You need rest."

"No. I am serious. I can picture it now. She's going to march… waddle… in here and act like she really cares, when all she wants to do is jump on our bandwagon… well, I say… she's not allowed. *No vay!*" she said trying to painfully shake her head from side to side.

"Hey, Mala did you take my mum to her AA meeting? Is she okay?"

"She's fine. Please don't worry. Do you need anything?"

Sharon was getting moody again, the drugs made her feel drowsy and her throat wasn't as strong as it was before, so she had the tendency to get agitated or flip out for no reason. She tried to shout but the roar was stuck. "Of course I need a few things. First, I want to get out of this bloody bed. I want my life back. My independence back. My car. My house. My bed. My job. Do you think it is pleasant for me to sit here and wonder what is going to happen in my life? I don't care if I have a lump in my throat. I'll be damn sure I don't die in this bloody bed."

"Calm down Sharon, please. This is not good for you. You are not going to die," Mala was pleading again.

"We are all going to die."

"Yes, I know, but not yet."

"You don't bloody know that for sure. Who says you decide when it's time for you to die? Unless of course you commit suicide, which is a cardinal sin."

"This is so morbid Sharon, and not getting us anywhere."

"So is this situation I am in now. I really don't want to be here Mala. If I am going to die, I would like to do it in my own home."

"But you're not going to die… yet. Not now, Sharon."

"Don't Sharon me. I know what is going on. I have cancer. Throat cancer. Do I look stupid to you?"

"No," Mala said trying to calm her down with her honey sweet almond eyes.

"Then stop treating me like I am stupid."

"I'm not Sharon. I promise I'm not."

"Yes you are. You never used to be like this with me. I'm not delicate you know. I can take anything that comes my way. Anything at all. Do you know that I am stronger than all of you? Mum, Washington, Noor and everyone put together. Did you know that?"

"Yes."

"Good, then stop pretending that I'm weak. Just be my friend."

"Okay." Mala knew her best friend was feeling useless and extremely frustrated. "I'm going downstairs to get a drink. Do you want anything while I'm down there?"

"Yes! Get me a bloody fag."

"How the hell can you think of smoking at a time like this? Are you thick?"

"No! I'm not thick. I'm stressed!"

Mala gave her friend the ugliest dirty look and said. "Bye Sharon," as she walked out the door in a huff.

Sharon tried to watch TV, but she couldn't concentrate. She wanted to talk. After all, she didn't really know how much longer she would have a voice. So, she tried to strike up a conversation with the boy next to her. It was torturous. He had moved into the two thousand square foot ward with Sharon the previous night. They had their own space and the room was large. It was like two private, open flats facing each other. Only in this case, medical supplies, props and machines, decorated the space.

"So, where are you from?" Sharon inquired.

"England."

"That's nice, what do you do here?"

"Nothing."

"That's even nicer," Sharon said with absolute sarcasm and with a roll of her beautiful green eyes. "So, why are you in here, if you don't mind me asking?"

"Nothing."

"I see." Sharon sat up in her bed and stared at this insolent looking man, who had a boyish dissatisfied look on his face. "Looks like nothing has got you into a mess. It's a harsh world out there isn't it mate. It's usually *something* that puts us in hospital."

Silence.

"Do you have family here?" Sharon inquired.

"No."

"Who are those people who come and visit you?"

"Nobody."

"Negativity is very bad. If you put out positive vibes into the atmosphere, you will get whatever you put out a hundred fold. So, if your life is full of *nothingness* and *nobodies*, then I guess that is what you are. A *nothing* and a *nobody*. Right?"

"Yes."

"Do you ever make functional sentences when you speak?"

"No."

"Why?"

No answer.

"Helloooo?"

No answer.

"You are such a boring chap. I am so sorry to have bothered you." Sharon picked up her magazine and started reading an article on David Beckham and Posh Spice. It was so boring, it was making her fall asleep. Before she dosed off, Neil walked into the room.

"Sharon, my beautiful flower, you look fabulous." Neil was a character who had the thick body of a cartoon character similar to *Johnny Bravo.*

"Piss off Neil," Sharon said with a half-smile. "I heard you replaced me already. How could you do that?"

"Nah nothing like that. You take your time. Take as much time as you need. We are fine there."

"You know I'll be out of here in no time right?"

"Like I said Shaz, you take your time. All the children say hi, especially Jun Do. He misses biting ya Shazzer."

"Oh bloody hell Neil. Did he get sorted out with his drugs?" Sharon felt connected when she was talking about school with Neil.

Neil started to giggle. "Yeah, they are giving him a higher dose of what he was on before… blimey what are they trying to do? Make the boy bite harder? Listen, I have to run, we have Parents Day today. Just give me a shout if you need anything."

"Ahhhhhhhhhhhhhhhhhhhhhhhhhhhhhhh." Sharon was screaming at the top of her lungs. A very squeaky painful sound and vibration resonated from her throat. The nurse came rushing in like a bull.

"What's wrong Ms. Connell, are you feeling alright?" The poor nurse looked so concerned. She also didn't want Sharon disturbing the other patient in the room.

"Do I look like I feel alright?" Sharon said meanly, rolling her eyes so far back into her head again, she looked like Linda Blair from *The Exorcist*.

"I'm not sure Ms. Connell. I heard you scream and thought you might need something," the nurse said as she checked all of Sharon's vital signs before moving swiftly to her chart.

Sharon finally looked at Neil and Said. "Bloody good service here if you ask me." She looked back at the nurse. "I don't need anything darling. I was testing out the vibrations in my vocal chords. I wanted to see and hear if I could still shout."

"I see." The nurse folded her arms. She was not the least bit impressed. "In the future, if you need anything please use the call button," she said as she walked briskly out of the ward. Mala was on her way in and the nurse had a very grouchy look on her face as she briskly exited the ward.

"Gosh, what's up with her, she looked like she wanted to kill somebody," Mala said as she placed her bag on the side chair.

"Yeah me," Sharon retorted like a kindergarten student.

Neil was in the corner giggling at the whole incident. "Listen Shaz, I've got to dash. Parents Day today..."

"Parents Day? I want to go. Can I come...?" said the queen of her own interrupted thoughts.

"Absolutely not!" Mala said, scrunching her forehead.

"Quiet Mala," Sharon said as she pressed the call button for the nurse. She came back in but with her arms folded this time. She was indifferent.

"Yes Ms. Connell. What is the problem now?"

"I want to leave for a few hours."

"That is impossible." The nurse was looking down at Sharon as she spoke, her folded arms high above her chest.

"Says who?" Sharon said indignantly as she folded her arms as well.

"Dr. Andrews."

"Tell him it's urgent."

"He's in surgery. Now, if that is all I can help you with, please get some rest because you have a very heavy day tomorrow. And it is impossible for you to leave." She walked out of the room and the boy next to her smiled. Sharon turned to him.

"Oh so, Mr. Nobody finds this funny does he?"

He didn't answer.

Neil left the hospital while Mala stayed with Sharon. Sandy came to the hospital in the late evening but Sharon had already fallen asleep. When Washington came to visit with Alex it was very late. He picked up Mala and took the train back to London.

The next morning Sharon woke up for her first treatment of chemotherapy, and felt very sick afterwards. She kept on vomiting and falling in and out of consciousness.

The only thing she said to her mother and Mala was, "Please get me out of here."

Chapter 37

South East Asia

Craig was partying almost every day. He liked the atmosphere and he had met so many women in the past month. He couldn't believe he was thinking about leaving Asia. He received another email from Sophia that morning. He didn't reply. He didn't want her anymore.

Dave called to speak to him about the situation and tried to understand what happened between them. And all Craig said was it wasn't Kismet. They were not meant to be. Dave wanted to call Sophia and tell her to cease the emails, but decided to let his petal deal with this one on her own. She had come full circle with the situation. It was clear as well as obvious that the universe sent Craig into her life to teach her a lesson.

One might have argued that it was a harsh lesson. Nevertheless, it was made by choice. Her journey gave her new meaning and fundamentally made her see that life must flow, although it can be so unpredictable. Owing to the situation between her and Craig, Sophia became stronger and indeed more receptive to everything around her.

It seems to be a universal rule through cultures and across time that, the end of something always brought promise for new beginnings.

.

Chapter 38

Surrey

Mala was getting prepared for her trip to Bombay. She found out that the climate was blissful, and the summers were colourful and steaming hot. London was also getting warmer again.

Sharon was still in hospital but the cancer had finally gone into remission. Her doctor told them the good news, but advised Sharon to stay for a few more days or a week for observations and follow up examinations.

It was Sunday evening and many visitors – close friends and students – hovered around Sharon's bed. She was looking healthy again and appeared to be in high spirits. Mala knew her trip abroad was going to be much easier knowing that her best friend was going to be fine.

Mui Mui, Mrs. Cheung, Jun Do, Jun Do's mother, Washington, Alex, Neil, Sandy, Fatima, Benjamin and one of Sandy's friends from AA surrounded Sharon. It was wonderful to see her smiling and laughing again. Her throat was much better. She had lost all of her hair from the chemotherapy and Mui Mui's gift – a hat – was bright fuchsia pink with little orange sunflowers embroidered all along the sides. It was pink for love, orange for self-respect and willpower, and it was received with a heart-warming smile and stroke to Mui Mui's soft face.

"This is lovely precious. Thank you so much for the present." They definitely had a soul connection. It was true and real. It was obvious how much they missed each other.

Washington brought his bongos because Sharon had asked him to. "So, are you going to play for me or not?"

"Are we allowed?"

"Wait, I have to ask Mr. Nobody, next to me here, if he minds." He was with his family and he wasn't talking to them at all. A lady, who looked slightly older than him, was sitting on a chair reading a book. And a man who looked like it was his father was on the sofa reading a magazine on carpentry. They had no interaction with each other.

"Hey… Mr. Nobody, would you like to join the party? You have to meet Mr. Washington Cannelli of La Bella Luna. He is amazing. He just came back from Cannes, and will be sailing us around on a yacht soon." Sharon was doing some stellar PR for Washington.

The boy insipidly looked over at Sharon and said. "Sure."

"What about your family? Ask them to join us. You are boring the crap out of them Mr. Nobody. Look at them sitting there. Look what you've done to them. They have nothing to say to you. You have made them into nobodies that's why they have nothing to say."

The woman looked up from under her book. She definitely looked like a female version of *Inspector Morse*. She was smiling. She was so glad her brother was lying next to this flamboyant woman.

Sharon looked over at her and inquired. "So, you must be Mr. Nobody's…?"

"Sister. My name is Sophia Martin." She got up to shake her hand. "And this is my father Daniel Martin. And that over there is my brother Alister."

"So, you have had to deal with this young man for your entire life. I tell you, a month lying next to him has been the most boring experience any woman could imagine," Sharon said as she shook Daniel's hand. She then extended her hand out to the boy and said,

"Nice to meet you Alister. Finally, I can put a name to my sleeping partner. So Sophia, what do you do here?"

"Nothing."

"Oh bloody hell! Your family must be really into nothing-ness," Sharon said rolling her eyes again.

"Well, I was in Asia, and then decided to move here, to be close to my father and help this one here." Sophia was looking right at Alister. "Hong Kong was terrible."

"I'm from there you know, my dad, Mr. Connell was a famous jockey. Wow, what a small world," Sharon was beaming.

Both, Sharon and Sophia felt like the world was under one roof today, like a cosmic force had pushed all of them together for some unknown reason... maybe not totally unknown.

"Okay ladies and gentlemen, please put your hands together for Washington Cannelli." Sharon was in very good spirits. She was clapping wildly, which made everyone stop and listen.

Washington began singing and Alex joined in. It was like a small make-shift samba party in ward 332 that night. Everyone was dancing, laughing, smiling, eating and praying for Sharon to get better. Dr. Andrews and "Nurse Bitch" were there, having a good time too.

Sandy Connell couldn't ask for anything more. Her prayers were finally answered.

Daniel Martin couldn't ask for anything more either, because his prayers were finally being answered too.

Both parents had a glow about them that could only be recognised through the blessing of parenthood.

Chapter 39

London

Mila was in London. It was almost time for them to go visit their mother. She was staying in Hammersmith with her sister before their departure.

Mila wanted to buy some civilised toiletries and had hinted at Maneck staying at Mala's and Washington's flat for two days. Mala was not impressed with the request and was speaking to Mila with her eyebrows perched very far up her hair line. She was not interested in Maneck's flighty, irresponsible ways. It was clear to her, he was back to his old habits again. He was not happy that Mila was leaving and had asked his mother to look after their children while she was away.

Mila asked Mala if she was sad to leave Washington and Mala revealed that she had a deep sadness in her heart, because a part of her wanted him to ask for her hand in marriage and the other part was scared of pressuring him into doing something he didn't want to do. Deep down inside she wished he would someday make their love legal. But... was there such a thing as legal love? Love is free and has no boundaries.

Mala needed to get a few last minute things too but decided to get them the next day. The hospital was so far away and she was tired of travelling to Surrey every day. Nevertheless, she knew she had to make the journey up there to say bye to her precious Sharon.

When she got there, Alister and Sharon were chatting about the wrestling on TV. Alister was cheering for Atomic Alice and Sharon was cheering for Tankhead Teresa. They looked like a married couple. Their friendship was something medication couldn't buy. It was the best treatment for both of them and all their sarcastic ideologies about life.

"When are you out of here my darling?" asked Mala.

"Dr. Andrews says I can definitely leave next week," Sharon's attention was on Tankhead Teresa.

Alister looked over at Sharon. "I am really going to miss her. Miss Reality Check over here. I have to be here for another five weeks." Alister was still bound to the bed and wheelchair. It was taking so long for the muscle memory in his legs to re-engage.

"Why so long?" Mala asked.

"Still have trouble walking," Alister said as he massaged his legs.

"*See vot drugs does to people,*" she said shaking her head from side to side like an Indian aunty.

"*See vot smoking does to people?*" Mala began shaking her head with true Indian aunty precision.

"Are you excited, Mala, about leaving for India?" Sharon asked.

"Yes and no. I'm a bit nervous."

"Has Washington popped the question already?"

"No," Mala sighed.

"What? Why not? What is he afraid of?"

"Me." She sighed again.

"Oh come on Mala, that's absolute rubbish and you know it. What's the real excuse?"

"I can't put my finger on it. It's always about money. But that can't be it. Can it?"

Alister interrupted. "Men are scared of commitment."

"Men are from another bloody planet. It's embarrassing," Sharon retorted. "Look at us. We are so old already, and acting like silly teenagers, waiting around for someone to marry us, especially someone who's been around for eighteen years. Blimey!"

"He will ask me when the time is right," Mala responded nonchalantly.

"Are you sad?" Sharon asked looking a bit worried.

"No."

"Angry?"

"No."

"How do you feel?"

"I'm trying to feel balanced. I have told him what I want, and if he's not ready, then what can I do? I have to see my mother and that's the only thing on my mind right now."

Sharon, Alister and Mala chatted for two hours about cancer, heroin, love, marriage and South East Asia. Sharon and Alister clearly had developed an amazing bond and friendship within a short time. They both grew up in Hong Kong and met in Surrey. What an intensely small world.

"Sharon, I have to go. I'm so tired," Mala said as she yawned with a big noise similar to her father's yawn. Sometimes he would add a melody to it, to make the yawn more socially acceptable.

"Okay, go precious. Call me when you get there, to INDIA! You are really going back to your roots *auntyji*."

Mala bent down to kiss Sharon on the forehead and give her a hug. "I will be back soon."

"Take your time *bungy*. I'll be here. Go on then…" Sharon didn't want to start crying. She was going to miss her best friend so much. She felt a small void in her heart opening up. She visualized it getting smaller instead of bigger. Mala was about to walk out but she called her back. "Mala… Thanks…" she said as she began to cry.

"For what?"

"Everything my sweet Indian *auntyji.*"

"Awww… don't say that Sharon. My only wish was for you to get better."

"*And your vish came true aunty,*" she said as she bobbled her head from side to side. "Please have fun and most importantly take care of yourself."

"*I vill aunty,*" Mala said as she came back to give Sharon another hug.

At 8:30 p.m., Mala got home and Washington was there. Mila was probably with Maneck.

"Hey, lover, why aren't you at work?"

"I wanted to spend time with you."

"You're so sweet Washington."

He had prepared a candlelight dinner for them. Tea lights on the breakfast bar shone with fervour. In the middle of the table was a bright cherry red heart-shaped candle radiating with the impression of hope.

They ate and talked, but still there was no mention of a marriage or a proposal. Two bottles of wine later – in Mala's stomach and swirling around in her head – Washington spoke up.

"Mala."

"Yes."

"There is something I need to tell you."

"Yes."

He sighed, pulled her towards the sofa and spoke, "Mala."

"Yes."

"There is something I need to tell you."

"Yes." She was getting nervous, she didn't know if it was the happy or sad kind.

"I have thought so much about us this past week… and I have

felt an empty space in my heart… the thought of you leaving… something inside me feels like…"

"Like what?" Mala interrupted.

"Like silence… and this silence is killing me."

"I don't understand," she said frowning.

"You know… I promised… I would ask for your hand before you leave."

"Yes, I remember."

"And now the time has come…" he looked away in shame.

"You can't do it."

"No… it's not like that," he pleaded.

"It's okay Washington."

"Would you marry a man who has no money… or who doesn't have as much money as you?"

"Is it about money again, because you're not getting to the point."

"Okay… okay… I'm… I'm not ready…"

Mala's heart sank to the bottom of her soul which suddenly felt like a barren well. Her instincts were haywire today. Part of her thought he was going to propose to her, which would have made her the happiest woman in the world. However, another part of her heart seemed to beat to the tune of Washington's drum, the part of her that resonated with the sting of rejection. She didn't cry nor was she mad. She placed a languid kiss on his forehead and said. "I understand." She didn't know what else to say. What else was there for her to comprehend?

For Mala, love was all they needed.

For Washington, it was about more. He wasn't materialistic. He just wasn't ready.

How does one explain readiness? Does anyone really know? It could be sparked by a song, something a friend whispers, a light breeze, or even the deep scent of perfume wafting around the city.

Washington realised that men have a difficult way of expressing themselves. He could see the hurt and loss in Mala's eyes. He reached into the depths of himself; he couldn't quite put his feelings into words. All he knew was that he needed a bit more time.

Mala and Washington made tender love that night. His strong hands grazed her womanly thighs, hands intertwined. The thought of her was not fabricated. He adored her. She was his everything. At the end they lay in each other's arms and cried, just like the first time eighteen years ago.

In the morning, Mala woke up and was running around London like a headless chicken; she needed and wanted to say goodbye to so many people.

Bazica was first on the list, but ended up becoming last. When she got there her heart skipped about a hundred beats. She couldn't believe what she saw. As a matter of fact, upon reflection, Mala wasn't the least bit surprised. The scene was typical. Noor was sitting with Ahmed in her usual spot.

Fatima caught her eye, but Mala mouthed to her, "I'll be back later." Fatima replied with a subtle nod.

Next, she proceeded to High Street Kensington to bid *adieu* to Master Kamal. She bought him an incense holder and a packet of 100 Flavours incense sticks. He encouraged her to '*Keep moowing with yoga,*' since she was obviously benefiting from it. He passionately revealed to her that he could undoubtedly see a change in her.

She passed by Boots and picked up her favourite shampoo, conditioner, foam wash and body cream, all in the scent of vanilla cream. She loved smelling like a bakery. Afterwards, she got on the train and made her way to see Sandy.

"Hiya, lovely lass."

"I wanted to say goodbye… well… not goodbye… see you soon."

They both had a cup of coffee in Shepherd's Bush and talked about Sharon and how much Sandy owed her recovery to Mala's positivity.

"I bought you a present lass, to make sure you brighten up the city." She pulled out a bright yellow bikini with a matching sarong. The lemon yellow ensemble was so bright, it was almost neon.

Mala was giggling with delight. They parted, with a feeling which made both of them trust that someone, somewhere, from some religion, up in the heavens was listening to them.

Finally, her last stop was Bazica. The place where so much began and ended.

She brought Fatima a demo tape of Washington's music, since she had never been to La Bella Luna. Her father would have died of a belly flop and screamed blue murder if he ever found out Fatima had visited a bar, lounge, disco or any other venue echoing 'fun.'

She bought Benjamin a mug which read, '*I will always work overtime – I even made my own coffee today.*' Mala couldn't think of anything else to get him.

"Thank you so much for this Mala," Fatima said warmly.

"I hope you like it, and I'm so sorry that I had to dash off earlier. Do you think your father will let the two of us sit down and have a coffee together? Can you tell him that I'm leaving and I just want to sit and have a quick chat and say goodbye?"

"Yes, for sure Ms. Mala. I'll go get your cappuccino and come right back. I'll just have a quick word with him and my mother, to let them know I'll be off for a bit."

While Fatima was talking to her father, Mala sat down at her favourite table – the one she and her two friends shared, halfway under the beige canopy and halfway on the sidewalk. It was getting warm again and the air was comfortable. Fatima finally sat down.

"So, what happened with Noor? What is the deal? Why are they here? What were they talking about?" Mala sounded like a menopausal teenager again.

"They were talking about her weight. And Ahmed was complaining how fat she had become…"

"I must say that she has become ferociously bigger." Mala admitted. "You didn't mention anything about Sharon did you Fatima?"

"Not in so many words."

"What does that mean?"

Fatima sipped her hot chocolate. "She asked me where both of you were, and I said Sharon was sick and you were leaving. The silly woman didn't even want to know more. All she wanted to do was talk about herself. After Ahmed yelled at her, he stormed off and he left her crying like an idiot. Again. So I sat with her and comforted her."

"Wow that sounds like typical Annabelle Noor. What did she say?"

Fatima cleared her throat. "It goes something like this. Annabelle and Ahmed are moving back to London, because she hates working at Café Des Artistes and Ahmed went bankrupt."

"Is that it?" Mala asked.

"No there is more. Anna Maria and Annabelle had a huge blow out because something went wrong at the restaurant. Something along the lines of some money going missing. And the hiring and firing of staff. Anyways, Mr. Noor had a special dinner for the Rotary Club of Paris and that's when Annabelle lost it…"

"Not her weight obviously," Mala interjected.

Fatima was laughing as she continued. "And so the story goes, that she started swearing and yelling at Anna Maria, in the kitchen. Her father, and obviously her friends, heard the ruckus and he barged in and told both of them to keep quiet. So, Annabelle starts crying and Anna Maria is in the corner with her arms folded, looking at Annabelle like she is a ten year old brat having a tantrum. Annabelle goes off on her speech about how Anna Maria is a whore, a good for nothing French tart who steals money from her father."

"WOW!" Mala was speechless. Her mouth hung open as she enunciated the last "w" of the word.

"It gets worse. She then picked up a piece of steak, which in Ms. Noor's words had obviously been marinating in red wine, pepper, garlic and capsicum for the whole day – and then picks it up, out of the Tupperware, and throws this piece of raw steak at Anna Maria."

Mala was in fits of laughter. She was cackling like a hyena, holding her stomach and almost falling off her chair. Fatima was laughing too.

Mala wiped away the tears of humour from her eyes and said. "Please go on, this is getting ludicrous as well as hilarious!"

Fatima continued, "Then her father kicks her out of the restaurant, politely, because his friends were there, and told her that they would speak later. That night, when she got home, she wasn't apologetic. She wanted revenge and her father knew it. So to appease her, he gave her ten thousand pounds and shipped her back here to London for a while to cool off. In the meantime, Ahmed was watching his money suddenly roll out of his pocket because of an unpredictable new stock. He and his brother had put all of their inheritance into that one stock."

"Tragic and very dramatic. I wouldn't expect anything else from Noor."

And like a youngster, Fatima hastily said, "If you do speak to her, please don't mention any of this to her."

"Don't worry Fatima, I won't. I'd probably crack up in her face first. This is all probably material and drama for her book. It's so funny." Mala started laughing again.

"It is very comical. And how is Ms. Sharon feeling?"

"Much better, when she gets out you have to tell her the whole story." Mala was still laughing. "What about you? What happened to this mysterious boyfriend of yours?"

"Dumped him." Fatima sighed. "He wasn't what I was looking for." She looked over at her parents who were working the floor of Bazica like robots. "And he wasn't Lebanese."

"I see." Mala sounded like an *aunty* again.

They talked for a little while longer about Noor's big arse and how she completely, absolutely and obviously let herself go. And how Ahmed had turned from a looker into a farmer.

Sharon was right again. Some of them were moving forward and the rest had no clue.

Fatima wished Mala well and hoped she would have a good time. "I'll see you soon."

"*Ciao* Fatima." With that, she left Bazica – her sanctuary of *auntydom*

That night, Mala went to La Bella Luna to watch Washington play. She saw Alister's sister sitting in the booth she always sat in. Starring at the boys play, Mala didn't know who Sophia was looking at. It could have been any of them – Alex, Rodrigo or maybe even her Washington.

Sophia was blushing. "I'm here to see… Alex… I bumped into him at the hospital the other night, after you left and he asked me to come down."

"That's great. Do you like it here? And how did they convince you?" Mala said as she took a seat in the booth next to Sophia.

"I love it here. It was Sharon who convinced me… she did all the work." Sophia was smiling.

"Sharon is a miracle, isn't she?"

"Yeah, my brother adores her."

The set was amazing that night, music filled the air and when Washington caught Mala's eye, he played like he had never played before. It was like an audible life stream pulsating through every molecule in Mala's body. She was going to miss Washington with all her heart. He was the love of her life.

Chapter 40

London

"Hurry up Mila!"

Mila was in the bathroom patting her eyes dry. She had been crying all night. Maneck had been with her last night and was as high as a kite through his snorts and sniffles as he tried to, in his mind, comfort Mila. He had no clue how to be a husband or a father, but Mila still loved him unconditionally.

Mala had tried to tie up all her loose ends except for the Montessori school. They were not pleased at all with her swift departure. She should have informed them earlier, but she didn't. The principal, Mrs. Haymoth, gave Mala a lecture on responsibility. She was a 78 year old powerhouse, so Mala didn't mind. What she did mind was when Mrs. Haymoth suggested that Mala had no compassion for the children and that her departure would slow down the progression of their learning curve. She couldn't remember the rest after that; she simply wasn't interested in getting wrapped up in Mrs. Haymoth's guilt trip.

Saying farewell to her students was tough though. Simran cried so much. Her students had made her a big quilt with their pictures and hand prints on it, and wrote a saying or a word about Teacher Mala. Timmy's was the cutest. He wrote, "Thank you for being an inspirational brown lady."

Mala didn't pack it in her suitcase, as it was too bulky. She hung it on her chair in the study facing her computer, with the tiara from her birthday still beaming like a beacon of light.

"Mila hurry!" Mala was getting impatient. Everything she began doing was in high speed motion.

"Washington, here is the rent for four months." She handed him the check. "Mila, I'm leaving without you if you don't hurry up."

Washington looked at the check. "Why so much? I thought you were only going for…"

"I don't know how long Washington, just in case… just think of it as cash for storing some of my stuff here. Where is that sister of mine… MILA!"

Washington was so embarrassed, but he knew he couldn't afford the rent on his own. He looked down at the floor.

"We're friends before anything else Washington, remember that."

He smiled.

Mila finally emerged from the bathroom looking like a raccoon.

"Are you ready?" Mala was agitated.

"Yes." Mila was still teary eyed.

Washington, Mila and Mala took a mini cab to Heathrow airport. In the car she remembered Ali. She had forgotten to say goodbye to him. She insisted on a quick diversion.

At Bayswater, the minicab driver still had his engine running while Mala went to find Ali. He wasn't there. Sanjay was. He was so distinguished with his Oxford-Indian accent and stylish Western clothes. He was definitely a *desi*, like her. But something about him didn't appeal to her a hundred per cent.

"Sanjay, is your dad around?"

"No, how can I help you today? He has taken sick and I am replacing him in the shop today." He was so posh.

"Can you please tell him I said bye? I'm going on a long holiday, but I will be back very soon. Please give your dad my regards and a big hug from me."

"Will you be gone a long time?"

"A few months. I wanted to come by, so he wouldn't think I forgot about him or that I've stopped cooking Indian *khana*."

Sanjay smiled. "I will certainly pass on the message when I see him tonight. Perhaps Mala... when you get back we could..."

She didn't let him finish his sentence. "Bye Sanjay. See you soon." And off she raced back down the road to the minicab and sped down the motorway to the airport.

Washington was squeezing Mala's hand and she could feel his heart pounding against her head, which was on his chest.

The sisters checked in and were standing by the gate.

"Please come back soon, Mala."

"I'll try."

"And have a wonderful time."

"I'll try."

"Go with a light heart, princess."

"I'll try."

"Stop saying that, you are making me sad." Washington put his head on her shoulder. She moved slightly and kissed him passionately and whispered in his ear. "I am going to marry you one day Washington Cannelli."

He smiled at her and stroked her long jet black hair. "Me too Mala Amani."

They parted with ease and most importantly, as friends. Best friends.

The flight took fifteen hours. It was gruesome. Mala sat by the window and as the plane took off, London looked like a distant paradise of history – Mala Amani's history; one that could not be replicated by anyone.

Chapter 41

India

"Wake up Mala! Wake up, we're landing." Mala was snoring like an elephant as Mila shook her back into reality.

Mala awoke with the crusty residue of sleep still in her eyes.

"Gross Mala, wipe that stuff out of your eyes." Mila had a look of scorn on her face, as if she had swallowed something undesirable and the taste wouldn't go away. The same face she had when they were teenagers and disagreeing on something.

As the plane started its decent, Mala felt like a circus troop was performing in her belly: jugglers, tight rope walkers, acrobats, lions jumping through rings of fire and elephants parading around an entire awe-stricken audience. She didn't know if it was the turbulence from the flight or the excitement.

She peered out of the window and saw tiny squares of green paddy fields aligned in uniformed rows. The city looked fairly flat. As they approached Bombay International Airport, the lady on the overhead speaker spoke Hindi in a sing-song way, which sounded like a love song.

The voice changed and something made Mala pause. All the thoughts in her head ceased as the lady spoke. Before she knew it, it was time to disembark.

As the two sisters exited the plane, the heat hit them like a ton of bricks. It was sweltering hot and the humidity was crawling into the layers of clothes and skin, as beads of sweat emerged like tropical bubbles. Mila was already peeling off her London layers.

They stood in line at customs for forty five minutes. Indian people took life at an easy and comfortable pace, and it was blatantly obvious from the moment Mala and Mila arrived. The charm of the Indian people's attitudes already began to grow on these two Londoners.

As they walked out of customs into the arrivals hall, the circus in Mala's stomach started to act up again.

The automatic doors opened wide and they began their walk towards Durga. Visions of her mother in a pink sari swayed around in her mind and memories of her earthly beauty swam up from the depths of ancestry, filling a family bond of spirit. Mala was looking for the same pink sari, as it was the last thing they saw their mother wear before she disappeared – which felt like an eternity ago.

As they got closer, they saw her. She was alone. She was wearing a black and white floral summer dress. Her light brown hair was tied back into a short ponytail and her milky olive skin was shining with a touch of bronze. She was squinting to see if these two beautiful girls, walking her way, were really her daughters.

The closer they got, the wider her eyes opened and she began waving frantically. Her smile was nothing like Mala had seen before. Her mouth was as wide as the sky and her eyes beamed with more tenderness than Mala had ever seen. Tears of joy began to cascade down her face, spouting from her eyes and filling in the crevices near her nose. She wanted to sprint towards her daughters, but the security guard put his hand up so she couldn't get any closer.

Mala and Mila reflected all the joy back at their mother, and began running, with their trolleys, towards her.

"Mama!" both daughters screamed as they ran like two five year olds into her arms. The hair on Mala's neck stood up and felt like her heart swarmed into a gigantic organ taking over her entire being, like fractal energy. Lights and movements of vibrations encircled all three of them.

"*My babies!*" Durga couldn't let go of her daughters.

It must have looked like a scene from a movie, like the ones set in some other Asian country like Thailand, where a mother finds her two backpacker daughters after they have been in jail. The love and enthusiasm exuded by the Amani family made everyone stare. An American couple standing to the right of them was so happy that they too began to get teary eyed.

Mila heard the lady say, "Look at that Peter, isn't it amazing, Asians have so much passion for their kin."

"*Come... come... my Betis... let's go home.*" Durga had each daughter by her side and that was all she needed.

"My driver is coming. Hold on." She located the tiny man and when he saw Durga he folded his hands, as if in prayer, and greeted the three women with "*Namaste.*"

He took their bags and wheeled them towards her Mercedes. Mila and Mala looked at each other. They were both so impressed. Their mother wasn't struggling, and that was a blessing for them.

"Mama let me look at you." Mala couldn't stop staring at her. She indeed looked older, but her aura was fluttering and vibrating like the humming of whispering angel wings.

They got back to her five thousand square feet house, which over looked a golf course. It was amazing. Below her terrace was a resort-style swimming pool.

The house was spectacular. Yet, there was a simplicity about it. Even though it was big and spacious, the rustic furniture and wooden floors made it seem like a home rather than a mansion. Durga showed them their separate rooms. Mala's room was lavender and Mila's room was a light yellow hue.

After the grand tour, Durga and her daughters sat down for some spicy Indian *khana*. It was scrumptious.

The house manager/cook had outdone herself for the three women. It was the best Indian food they had eaten in such a long time, it tasted like home. Mintu, the house manager, had adapted well to their mother's Hindu-ness by never bringing beef into the house. Durga once referred to eating beef as sacrilegious when the women were much younger and this memory stuck in Mila's mind – that beef was like eating her mother. For Mala, it was another meat, enriched with the iron supplement she craved in her diet.

The array of tropical colours, smells and wonder wafted around them like sweet savoured memories of their childhood.

"I have a surprise for you girls." Durga couldn't believe she was referring to these two older ladies as girls.

"What is it Mama?"

"*Ve, just the three of us, are going on a cruise tomorrow.*"

"We are?"

"*Yaaa yaaaa… just the three of us… ve hawe so much to catch up on.*"

"Where is your husband?" Mila asked as she put a piece of rich supple mango in her mouth.

"*I sent him avay for a few days.*"

"What?" Mala was half laughing.

"*Yaaa… yaaa, ve have a wery sincere relationship. He understands Beti. Ve are wery old now.*"

"What a cool guy." Mala was impressed. She wanted to meet him.

The flight was exhausting and the excitement had worn Mala out. They had to get up early the next day so Mala retired first. Mila stayed up with her mother and gave her the rundown on her life and her grandkids.

That night, in her calm and peaceful lavender room, Mala dreamt of happy angels laughing on a cloud. Some were playing music, others were preparing food and the rest were talking. Beneath the cloud was a city. It wasn't anywhere on this planet, because it was made of gold; each and every person Mala knew was in this golden city, even her father. They all had brightly coloured rainbow wings attached to their bodies; the men wore crowns on their heads, and all the women had sparkling platinum tiaras above their heads.

She awoke at 4 a.m. and couldn't get back to sleep, so she went out to the terrace and did a few yoga stretches. The pool sparkled as the sun began to rise. She put on her bright yellow swimsuit Sandy gave her, which beamed symbolising intellect while the blue water bathed her in a healing whirlpool of truth.

She had so much to tell her mother, especially her feelings concerning Washington, but for now, she was in her element and she felt complete.

Chapter 42

London / South East Asia

Sophia was feeling calmer and secure in her new environment. She was adapting well. She didn't want to screw it up this time. She wrote Dave an email:

From: Sophia Martin

Dear Dave,

Alister is doing so much better and I think he has met a love interest at the hospital. Her name is Sharon Connell. A total far cry from Tanya. Sharon is short, boisterous... Irish... with red hair and green eyes. She is so beautiful. About a decade older than our Alister, nonetheless she has been amazing with my brother, she brings him down to earth all the time. I still haven't heard from Craig, and I don't think I am ever going to. I suppose it's been a blessing in disguise. Apart from Alister meeting someone at the hospital, *grandma-ma* has met someone too. I'm not sure if I'm falling in love or if it's the classic case of feeling lonely. Nevertheless, the attention is making me feel like an English Rose. He plays in a band at a restaurant called La Bella Luna. He is gorgeous. He is from Brazil and his accent is so intriguing. We might be going out on a date next week, depending on his schedule. I'm excited and look forward to hearing him speak. I know I said I liked the British accent, but my voyage has taken me elsewhere, somewhere more universal – are you impressed? You did teach me well my darling friend. If only you could see me now, you would have a lot to make fun of. I can't stop smiling. The other night he played a love song and dedicated it to me. I know, I know...mushy, soppy and wet. But being in London has made me feel softer and less tense than when I was back in Asia. Speaking of the Demon City, has anyone called about renting out Uncle Peter's flat? Please let me know; since I have not started work yet, the extra cash would be a big help. I have to start doing something soon, but I'm not sure what. Sharon Connell suggested I teach. I could never imagine myself around children. They frighten me. They might find me too pedantic and irkish. Please write soon and fill me in on everything. How's Sergio? Please say hello to him for me..

Love,

Sophia.

Dave received her email and wrote back almost immediately.

From: David Graham – *Christian Dior*

Dear Petal,

I am absolutely and certainly happy you have finally come to your senses. So have you slept with your Brazilian yet? You know what they say about Latinos. HOT. HOT. HOT. And HOT. Glad to know that Alister is better and he might be falling in love again. Try to help him not get trapped in a rebound relationship, because that would be the worst thing for him. As for Uncle Peter's flat, no one has inquired about it yet. I still have the keys, if you want I can go over and check to see if things are okay there. I hope your cleaning was enough Cinderella. Maybe no one wants to rent it because it smells like a graveyard in there. Whoops sorry, no pun or disrespect intended to Uncle Peter. And as for Sergio, well, the game is over. I should start practicing what I preach and not get bored so easily. He was too young for me and we both knew 'us' wasn't going to go anywhere. The next relationship I dive into I'm going to make sure that 'my little brother' stays in my pants before the first date. My problem is that I lust too much. More Prozac, more Prozac and more Prozac. Nah, just kidding. Work has been keeping me busy so, that's a bonus. Hopefully, I will come and visit you soon sunshine. But in the mean time you keep up the good work and stay away from irkland, it's much better here on earth, isn't it?

Love,

Dave

Chapter 43

India / London

Mila, Mala and Durga were on the cruise the next morning at ten. They were elated to be together. They were traveling around a few islands for five days.

Still, they hadn't got into the serious aspect of their lives. All of them were waiting for the other one to start. None of them appeared ready just yet.

Sharon was coughing again, but Dr. Andrews kept his promise, he was going to let her out in the next three days. He told her she had to come in twice a week for treatment and not work for a few months. He didn't want the cancer to emerge again.

Washington went to visit Sharon every day because he missed Mala so much and Sharon was his only connection to her. She kept giving him a hard time for not proposing to her and instead of feeling sad, Washington embraced her light-hearted bullying as humour.

Alex kept going with Washington, hoping he would bump into Sophia. With his hectic schedule, Alex didn't have much time to speak or to see her. After work every night he was so exhausted he passed out, and when he woke up it was time to work again. Today, he was hoping she would be there, because he had made an extra effort to wake up a little bit earlier before work. Washington made fun of him the entire way to the hospital.

"You take care of yourself Alister… I'll tell you what, you'll be seeing me twice a bloody week, for my bleedin' treatment. You better start getting better so you can bloody take both of us out when you leave this place." Sharon was trying to get his attention. But he was staring at the wall. "Hey, you going to act like Mr. Nobody again? Don't be so dramatic please Alister. It bores the living crap out of me. I'm sorry, I'm leaving here first, and getting on with my life, but we don't have to make this into a childish scenario. I'm way too old for this malarkey."

"Sorry," he said as he looked away from the wall and directly into her beautiful sultry green eyes. He was so happy he met her.

"Don't be sorry. We will all be fine in the end. And like I said, I promise I'll come and visit you every day. Before Mum gets here, do you want to go outside for a little bit?"

"Don't want to," he said sombrely.

"Come on Alister, don't be so pathetic. Let's go get some fresh air. I'll help you get into your wheel chair."

"No, Sharon I really don't feel like it."

"Suit yourself. Bloody try to be compassionate and what do I get? Nothing. I guess we are back to square one then aren't we?"

Sandy marched in with an empty suitcase. She was ready to take her baby home. She was ecstatic. "You ready doll?" She asked her daughter.

"Yeah mum, I really am. It's been too bloody long in here."

"I'm going to dump your things in here, then we can go." Sandy started packing while Sharon sat on the edge of Alister's bed.

"You know what the difference between me and you is Alister?"

"I'm a man and you're a woman."

"Don't be so bloody shallow mate! The difference is that I take life as it comes and situations as they emerge. If I got so wound up, or wounded, every time things didn't go my way, I'd be dead right now. Don't you want to play again?"

"No. Never." Alister was sulking again.

"Of course you do silly boy. Now, before I leave, I want you to promise that you'll get your act together and stop acting like a pouty child. It's boring and very unappealing. You're not looking so flash anymore mate. Especially when you act like that. I'm starting to lose interest. Whoops, look… there it goes oop… oop… woops… there it goes," she said as she looked at the sky as if her 'interest' was flying away. "There it goes again… flying… flying away," her green eyes looking straight up to the ceiling.

"Okay, Sharon, I get it… I'm not a baby," Alister said staring at her eyes.

"You're bloody acting like one." Sharon leaned over and gave Alister a big bear hug. "Imagine how it would be to walk again Alister. Think of that and you'll feel better in no time. I'll be back in a few days to see you again. I wouldn't want to miss another party in room 332."

Sharon got up and started towards the door, and she turned to Alister and waved goodbye. He blew her a flying kiss.

In the car, Sharon fell asleep. She had lost quite a bit of weight and was still weak. She was so glad to be out of hospital. Sharon was adamant that no aspects of her life would change. She wouldn't be able to dash around doing most of what she used to do before, but she was sure of one thing, she definitely needed stability and familiarity. If that meant people had to come to her, then Sandy was going to have to deal with it.

The next morning she woke up in her cold bed with a sore throat. Sandy begged Sharon to go back to the hospital to ensure there was no infection. But Sharon vehemently refused. She made it clear she wasn't going back until her next chemo treatment.

Mala was back on dry land. She was glad to be off the cruise. It was enjoyable because the three ladies laughed so much. However, the idea Durga had of the cruise was like the renditions Mala had in her mind of the *Love Boat* series, when the three of them used to watch when they lived in California. One could say that a part of the old Indian lady was waiting for Captain Stubing to greet her upon her arrival. Her daughters made fun of her the whole time and sang the Love Boat theme song every time the captain was in sight.

When they got back home, Mala remembered that Sharon had finally been discharged from the hospital. She couldn't wait to speak to her best friend. She knew she would be the happiest person on the planet. She dialled London.

"*Auntyyyyyyyyyyy*. How are you feeling?"

"Great. Mala. Great." Sharon was so excited to hear from her.

"You sound a bit rough... are you sure everything is okay?" Her yellow *chakra* started to twist a little bit. "Did you smoke?"

"No *bungy*, of course not."

"Are you sure?"

"Yeah."

Mala could hear the dishonesty in her voice. "Liar."

"Just one."

"Sharon I'm hanging up. You're useless. What the hell is your problem? Are you on a death wish? You're such an idiot." Mala's voice was getting increasingly louder and louder. She was getting increasingly impatient.

"I'm not on a death wish. I just wanted to see if I missed it."

"Do you?" Mala inquired in her best lecturing voice.

"No, not at all." Sharon was coughing. Again.

"So why the hell did you do it? What an idiotic way to prove something to yourself. Wasn't being in hospital for over a month not enough for you? Huh?"

"I lit it. I smelt it. And put it out. I swear it didn't even touch my lips."

"Pathetic, Sharon Connell. Did you actually learn something from your stupid, immature, dumb arse experiment?"

"I'll never smoke or be around a smoker ever in my life again. It was only a test."

"Stop testing yourself or anything else. You might end up dead." Mala was still irritated.

"You know, Washington came to see me almost every day since you've been gone."

"That is so sweet." Mala paused. "Does he miss me?"

"Tremendously, lass," Sharon said trying to imitate her mother's accent.

"Have you told your mum that you are living in sin and you want to get married?"

"He hasn't asked me yet." Mala sounded like her mother.

"Mala! You are going to sit there and have the nerve to talk to me about testing things out. Pathetic! You better make up your mind soon *bungy*! If you keep saying 'he hasn't asked me yet,' as a constant excuse to how much he loves you, or how much he wants to marry you, then you are going to lose him."

"I will talk to her. Soon." Mala sighed.

"When? And have you met your 'pink' step father yet?"

Mala was giggling. "No, she sent him away."

Sharon began giggling too. It was the same kind of laugh they shared at Bazica so many afternoons there together. "What do you mean she sent him away?"

"She wanted to spend time with us, so she asked him to go on holiday."

"I like it… a modern Indian lady."

"Sounds like a good title for a book, Sharon."

"Too plain, precious."

"My love, this is costing me a fortune. You know how it is here in the sticks. I'll call you next week to see how you are getting on with your treatment."

"Thanks precious. Take care. And talk to your *mamaji* quickly. You are really not getting any younger Mala."

"I will, I will."

"Bye love."

"Bye."

Mala returned to the living room. The sheer white curtains were pulled back and a gentle breeze floated in like a playful echo of freshness. The house was bright and airy with the sun rays that cheerfully embraced Durga's dwellings with a happy glow. It felt like the earth was whole and the heavens were smiling.

"Mama, I used the long distance again."

"*Is ewerything vell in London?*"

"Remember that girl Sharon, I was telling you about the…"

"*Smoker?*" Durga was pottering around the living room, re-arranging a painting of Buddha. He looked so peaceful.

"Yeah the one who has cancer?"

"*She should have stopped smoking no?*" she said, shaking her head from side to side.

"I know… I know ma… but I wanted to talk to you about something else."

"*That boy right… that boy you keep calling and keeps calling here.*" She stopped what she was doing, sat on the sofa and indicated for her daughter to do the same.

"Yes. And he is not a boy Mama, he is over 50, a little bit older than me."

"*Mala, he is…*"

"Please Ma, I'm begging you not to say that word again."

"*He's a…*"

"Wonderful man."

"*But he's black.*"

Mala sat closer to her mother on the enormous sofa. "I don't think that matters Mama."

"*I do.*"

"Why?"

"*It has newer vorked.*"

"Says who?"

"*Me.*"

"Mama I don't want to choose between you and him…"

"*Vould you?*"

"I don't want to." Her solar plexus began to vibrate with an uncomfortable resonance.

"*But, I am your mother.*"

"And Washington is someone I want to spend the rest of my life with."

"*Is there no Indian boy you like?*"

"No Mama, you don't understand… it's not about being Indian, or American or Black."

"*Then vot are ve talking about?*"

"Humanity."

"*Mala…*"

"Please Mama, let me finish saying what I have to say…"

"*You left home at such a young age and you don't hawe a foundation of family, that is vhy you think you lowe him.*"

"Ma, I don't want to get angry with you and feel like you are controlling me. And for your information we have been together for eighteen years. And I want to tell you how much this man means to me. He has been such an integral part of my life, and my life without him would be… grey. He brings so much beauty and colour to my life."

"*Vot does he do?*"

He's a musician."

"*Vot kind of life is that Mala? How are you going to support yourselves in your age?*"

"We will manage like a team."

"*I'm scared for you Beti.*"

"Why?"

"*Because you sound like me vhen I vas about to marry your father.*"

"You were eighteen Mama. I am so old now. Look at me."

"*Vhy does he lowe you?*"

"What do you mean? I don't know… I mean… it is some kind of connection we have. I can't explain it."

"*Do people in London look at you two vhen you are together?*"

"Sometimes."

"*How does that make you feel?*"

"It used to bother me, but now I don't care."

"*Thank God you don't hawe children… how vould people look at you… praise Lord Shiva…*"

"If I ever did have children, which I obviously can't now, I would hope that they would look at them as human beings before anything else and not label them because of the colour of their skin."

"*You still hawe the same fire in you Beti… same as vhen you vere a baby.*"

Mala saw a small smile creep up on her mother's face.

"*I must tell you… I am old fashioned and I don't agree vith this idea…*"

231

"You have to meet him."

"Vait… let me finish… I don't want to ever lose you or your sister again… and if it means that I hawe to go to Lord Shiva every day to pray… then you hawe all my blessings."

"What? Really? Mala was shocked. She wasn't expecting this kind of reaction. Her yellow *chakra* stopped making noise in her stomach and she felt like something was released. She felt warmth in her heart and the blockage was suddenly cleared.

"Yes Beti, I can't bear the thought of you or Mila not in my life again… I vould really die."

"I was so worried Mama."

"Don't cry Beti. I hawe made so many mistakes in my life… I can't begin to explain how many nights I hawe cried knowing that I vasn't there for you. I feel so much shame for abandoning you and Mila, that I almost killed myself. So I vouldn't have to deal with the pain or the rejection, vhich I could have received. But vhen I saw you girls… ladies, my heart felt like it started beating again. I became aliwe and human…"

"…But why did you tell us you were dead?"

"I don't know, I vas so frustrated at life and felt like I shouldn't hawe been given the chance of motherhood because I was putting you two through so much pain." She began to sob. *"And vhen Santosh did that awful thing to me, a part of me died. I vas veak and unable to function. So, I left California after six months and came back to India, to live with my mama and papa. Vhen I got the courage I mowed back to California and met Stewe. He got transferred back to India, and ve have been married for fifteen years."*

"Mama don't cry."

"And you don't cry Beti. There is no need to cry anymore. Crying is good sometimes, but ve all must stop it now."

"I forgive you, I was never angry at you, I was so worried about you all the time, and when Santosh told me you died, I felt like God had taken you away from us, because we had been bad and rebellious children… you don't know how much I blamed myself for always talking back to him."

"He deserved it."

"But you didn't deserve any of the repercussions of his temper reflected by his attitude."

"But look at you now my beautiful angel, look how much you hawe accomplished… and look how free you are…"

"I know, I am even going out with a Kharo!"

"Mala!"

"Oh Mama, I don't ever want to lose you again. I want us to be a family again and be happy."

"Let's do that."

"As of today… we will make this day, like a rebirth… all of us will start again as a new family. Me, you, Mila, Steve and possibly Washington… oh yeah and Maneck. You have to meet your grand-children. They are amazing."

"Yes… that sounds great Mala, you are a vise soul. Vot is your boyfriend's name? Vashington?"

"Washington, Ma."

"Haaa haaaa, like the state in Amrikkka?"

"Sort of Ma, Washington, not Vashington."

"Vell, if he is going to be in a Sindhi family, he is going to have to get used to being called Vashington. Ve could give him an Indian name no? Like Vashi? No?"

Mala laughed as she hugged her mother. "Thank you Mama for being so understanding. I was so upset when I spoke to you on the phone in London and we…"

"It's in the past Beti. And every day is getting better and better. We have to beliwe that. Today is the first day of our liwes, and ve vont dvell anymore. Ve are here together now, and that is vhat ve hawe to focus

on. Na Beti, just because I said yes to Vahsington, I don't vant you to go running back to London right away. I vant you to stay with me for a vhile longer okay Beti? Please?"

"Of course Mama"

"And money... you..."

"No... you don't worry. I suppose we have to thank Santosh for helping us out in that department."

"And for helping me hawe the two most beautiful daughters in the vorld."

Mila came up from the pool soaking wet. Durga beckoned for her to come to the sofa. She hugged her daughters tight and thanked Lord *Shiva* for keeping her angels safe while she was away.

Chapter 44

India

Relief. Mala felt relieved. Everything, once again was on a solid path. 'No more curves, please angels, please universe, please God.' She thought to herself.

She was sitting in a lotus position as she spoke to herself, and she was joyful as she imagined a golden cylinder of light traveling through her body.

She had already been in India for nine weeks and was loving it. The heat was helping her brown subtle skin glow and the mentality of the local people were giving her hope.

The phone rang and rang like an irritating sound of a whining animal. It was so loud and reverberated around the whole house, so everyone could hear. Mintu was at the wet market and Durga wasn't home either. She took Mila shopping for some paintings. Mala had chosen not to go. Today, she needed to be alone. Also, she was waiting for Washington's phone call to tell him the good news about how understanding her mother was and how she had aged into a beautiful, graceful woman.

She sneakily looked at her watch, as the cylinder of light disappeared from her visualization. It wouldn't be Washington, it was too early. He called at the same exact time every day. So, she continued with her yoga practice and let the phone continue to ring.

Ten minutes later, and twenty five *surinamaskars* and sun salutations later, the phone rang again. It still wouldn't have been Washington, but she answered anyway.

"Hello?"

"Mala."

"Washington, my love," She was in high spirits and so relaxed. "I'm so glad to hear from you. How are you? You called early today. How is everything? I have so much to tell you…"

"Mala…"

"Yes, Washington, is everything okay?"

"Mala…" His voice was shaking.

Silence.

"Hello… Helloo… Washington… what's the matter, you're worrying me."

"It's…"

"What is it? Washington, please stop joking around, you are making me feel so uncomfortable right now."

"It's Sharon…"

"What happened? Is she in hospital again?"

"No."

"Oh. Thank God."

"Mala, wait…"

"WHAT?" She started to panic.

"She's…"

"What Washington… what… what… what!"

"Dead."

As if in one single moment; the golden cylinder of light through Mala's body turned into a rusty, old beam of over-used energy. Her frequency and energy was no longer high; in a second, it had shrank to dust. She was depleted, and above all else, devastated. Her heart beat travelled to her throat and she vomited all over the receiver. She was groaning in pain. The vomit had shot up to her mouth so quickly. "Ahhhhahh… I can't breathe Washington… I can't breathe…"

"Take it easy baby… take it easy," he said as both of them were sobbing on the phone on two different sides of the planet.

"And Sandy?" Mala was shaking like a leaf.

"She won't speak to anyone. She's in a different world…"

"Oh Washington." Mala had never cried so hard in her life. "What happened? She seemed fine, I was speaking to her once a week, and she was great."

"Actually Mala, she went into surgery two weeks ago. She asked me not to tell you, she didn't want to worry you. The cancer spread to her lungs."

Mala couldn't ask the next question without feeling like she had walked onto a movie set again and had forgotten all her lines, all her movements and all her senses. "Did she… pass away… in the hospital?"

"No baby, it wasn't during treatment, it was in her sleep. She couldn't breathe. Sandy tried to wake her up this morning… but… nothing."

"Oh Washington…" Mala's vomit was all over the floor, the receiver, all over herself; all she could do was slump onto the floor like a heap of human flesh. She couldn't speak anymore. All she managed to say was. "I'll be there soon."

She hung up the phone and locked herself in the bathroom and began to wail like a lost child. She was punching her legs from frustration. Screaming, 'WHY. WHY. WHY?' She was so angry at the universe and everything humanity represented. She felt like every time her path was clear, another lesson was thrown in front of her, and she couldn't understand it. The whole year had been a mad roller coaster ride and finally it took the biggest dip. She vomited again, and again, and again.

As Durga and Mila entered the house all she heard was whimpering coming from the bathroom and the smell of regurgitated food engulfed her house. Durga knocked fiercely on the door while concerned in her racing thoughts.

"*Mala! Mala! Vot happened Beti? Open the door for Mama please.*"

"I'm okay Mama."

"*I can hear you are not. Now, hurry up and open the door. Vhy are you crying?*"

Mala opened the door. Crusty vomit was still all over her face and her eyes were bloodshot.

"*My God! Lord Shiva vot have you done to my Beti!*" Durga reached her arms out to her daughter and Mala wailed in her mother's arms. Durga patted her head.

"*Come and sit down. Tell me vot happened.*"

"She's D... D... D... dead."

"*Who?*"

"Sharon."

"*My God...*" Durga pulled her ears and started chanting a Hindu prayer.

Mila stroked her sister's shoulders and felt deep remorse.

"Mama I have to go back to London. I'm so sorry to do this but..."

"*It's fine Beti... Please stop...*"

Between sobs, "Thank you Mama."

"*Did you call Vashington?*"

Mala nodded.

Chapter 45

London

On the flight back to London, Mala took two Valium and fell into a thick black sleep.

She awoke with a freezing cold chill nestled in the back of her neck that wouldn't go away.

Washington greeted her at the airport. "My baby." He squeezed her with his strong arms and stroked her black hair. "I'm so glad you're back. Everything is going to be fine. I promise."

They took the train to Hammersmith. Mala felt like she was going to wake up soon, and that this hellish feeling encircling her would vanish.

Sandy was waiting for Mala when she got home.

"She's gone... my daughter is gone... someone didn't hear us Mala... someone took her away... Why!?" Sandy hadn't spoken in twenty four hours and she was quivering. Every inch of her was trembling with fear.

Mala took her hand and led her to the breakfast table. They sat on the stools. "I am so sorry Ms. Connell. I'm so sorry."

"Why did this happen to me, lass? I'm not a terrible woman."

"Please don't think like that Ms. Connell. You are not a horrible woman." Mala was crying again. The tears had a life of their own, releasing at the thought and memory of Sharon.

"She was my focus, my strength, my armour and now… I've been stripped."

"Oh Sandy. Please don't cry anymore… please… Sharon would have hated to see you like this." She buried her head on Sandy's shoulders.

After what seemed like years, Sandy finally calmed down and had a cup of tea. "She made us something before she left." Sandy took out three books. Two photo albums and a baby book. Mala remembered when they went shopping together for these items. Now, it was clear why she had made the purchase. Did Sharon Connell know she was going to die so soon? No one would ever know.

"I'm sure she would have wanted us to look at these together," Sandy said as she opened up the first page of the baby book.

It read:

Dear Mum and my best pal and favourite auntyji in the whole world, Mala,

Inside these books you will find distinct memories of life situations which changed my existence because you were both in it.

ENJOY! ENJOY! ENJOY!

I will be waiting for you – smiling – and in the meantime bloody watching over you.

Love,

Sharon

Sandy turned more of the pages with pictures of her daughter, as a toddler, which made her smile. Mala opened one of the photo albums and on the first page Sharon wrote:

Once upon a time there was a vhite aunty… And the rest is history… laid deep in the roots of our past. Live for now, for that will set you free.

Underneath a picture of Sharon smiling like a jewel. As Mala turned the pages, love, truth and humour filled her soul. Each picture told a story, beginning with their third or fourth coffee at Bazica nineteen years ago. The last picture was Sharon in room 332 with all of her friends and family before she passed.

Chapter 46

London

Saturday morning – Mala was wearing all black as she, Washington and Alex made their way to the funeral.

She woke up at five in the morning to write a eulogy for Sharon. Sandy requested that Mala speak at the church. Everyone she knew was there. Hundreds of people came to see her one last time. She was so loved.

Mala got up to say a few words to her best friend.

"Ladies and gentlemen, friends and family, we are here today, not to mourn the death of a person, but to celebrate the privilege that we have had, to come across such an inspirational being called Sharon Connell.

"Some of us have known her for decades, years, months or even just weeks. Yet, no matter how we have made contact with her, it is clear that she has made a tremendous impact on our lives. She must be smiling now, to see how much love she received throughout her life. She gave something to everybody here because she was real.

"Sharon Connell should be remembered as a risk-taker, someone who never became a slave to the past or a martyr for the future, because her philosophy to soldier on through the moment is the reason why we are all here this morning.

"I remember one day we were sitting in Bazica, our regular haunt, and she said, 'life is like a painting.' Inside this painting, routine and everything familiar made her safe. She then said that she had made a decision that life cannot be confined to just that one painting, because it was too bloody boring.

"On my way to Asia to visit my mother, she said to me, 'step out of the frame Mala; if you don't like it, you can always come back, because that colourful image of life will always be there waiting for you no matter what happens.'

"Her patience and truthful demeanour has helped all of us step out of that frame and given us a smile, a word, or a gesture of hope.

"So, in the words of a phenomenal human being, thank you for all the 'bloody' wonderful things you have inspired us to do in our lives. We love you Sharon Connell. May your soul rest in eternal peace. Thank you."

Mala looked into the sea of faces. She saw Alex holding Sophia's hand. Alister standing up in front of his wheel chair. Ms. Cheung hugging Mui Mui. Washington smiling and Sandy standing with her ex-husband and two other children.

Through death, there was life.

Mala stepped down from the podium and Washington took her hand. They started to walk towards the door.

"Mala, I know this may be an awful, awful time, or maybe not, because Sharon would have loved to see this. Mala... will... you..."

She didn't let Washington finish his sentence. She looked up to the sky and said "this is for you Sharon Connell." She then looked over at Washington and said, "Yes I will."

As they walked out of the church, Mala saw Noor and Ahmed. She was writing vigorously in a notepad. "Mala, I came as soon as I heard."

Mala hugged all thirty five pounds more of her, "I hope you are well Noor. Please keep in touch. Life is so short."

"Yes, I will. I promise I will. I know this might be a bad time, but can I ask you a few questions… I need it for my…"

Mala turned sharply at her. Washington still had his arms protectively around her waist. "If you are going to say anything about a book Noor…"

"How did you know?"

"Annabelle Noor, you are the most predictable human being on the planet. Now, if you'll excuse me. My fiancé and I have a few things to do."

"Fiancé?" Noor looked scornfully at Ahmed.

"Yes, put that in your book Noor. Goodbye."

Mala and Washington got home and felt exhausted. A deep void without Sharon somehow made them even closer. He placed the ring on the coffee table. The box was opened and the diamond was sparkling.

"This is as romantic as it gets princess." He got down on one knee and said, "Mala Amani, will you be my wife?"

"Yes Washington Cannelli, I will."

"In this life time and the next and the next and the next?"

Mala was smiling… finally. "Let's get through this one first."

He slid the ring on her finger and they went out for a romantic meal. They talked about Sharon Connell the whole night.

Chapter 47

Somewhere in the Universe... / London

So, how did it all begin? No one really knows where anything begins or if anything ever truly ends.

The next morning, Mala woke up. The sun was shining and the diamond, beautifully sized, sat unflawed on her finger.

She went into the study, let out a gigantic breath; switched on her computer, placed the tiara on top of her head; stared at her manicured white finger nails and began to type. Her hands flowed across the keyboard like a concert pianist and thus began her process of ultimate healing:

Her name is...

The End / The Beginning

"So it was in the beginning, so it shall be in the end"

– Bob Marley

Glossary of Terms (alphabetically):

Beti: Hindi word for daughter.

Bungy: An Indian slang word meaning toilet cleaner, or a person who does not look appropriate with proper attire. Referring to someone of a lower cast in a derogative way.

Burka: A loose garment covering the entire body and having a veiled opening for the eyes, worn by Muslim women.

Cantonese numbers:

Yut: Cantonese sound for 1.

Ee: Cantonese sound for 2.

Samm: Cantonese sound for 3.

Say: Cantonese sound for 4.

Mm: Cantonese sound for 5.

Lok: Cantonese sound for 6.

Chut: Cantonese sound for 7.

Cheung Sum: Chinese dress made of silk, usually worn by women of high status.

Chicken Makanvala: Chicken curry made with Indian spices, consisting mostly of a sauce rich in butter. Usually eaten with naan bread or saffron rice.

Desi: Word derived from Sanskrit. Means 'one from our country'; a national opposed to a foreigner.

Fota: Hindi word for cardamom seeds.

Garam Masala: An aromatic mixture of ground spices used in Indian cooking, usually containing black pepper, cardamom, cinnamon, cloves, coriander, nutmeg, and turmeric.

Gweilo: Cantonese word for a Caucasian person. It actually means White Devil.

Hare Bapere: Indian slang for – Oh My Gosh!

Jeera: Hindi word for black cumin seeds.

Kali: Goddess of destruction. She is Laxshmi's counterpart. The dark side of the Goddess of light.

Khana: Hindi word for food or to eat.

Kharo: Derogative Hindi word for a very dark-skinned person.

Moti: Hindi word for fat person.

Nirvana: (Sanskrit: 'becoming extinguished' or 'blowing out') *Pali nibbana*, in Indian religious thought, the supreme goal of certain meditation disciplines; peace.

Pitaji: Hindi word for father

Puri: Indian puffed bread made with white flour and deep fried in oil. Usually eaten with lentils.

Raj Mahal Dhal: Black lentils made with black kidney beans.

Samosa: Indian delicacy made with puffed pastry and meat or vegetables inside.

Samsara: (Sanskrit: 'flowing around') in Indian philosophy, the central conception of metempsychosis: the soul, finding itself awash in the 'Sea of Samsara,' strives to find release (*moksha*) from the bonds of its own past deeds (*karma*).

Tai Tai: Cantonese phrase/slang for a woman who is extremely wealthy and has nothing to do all day but shop and go for lunch.

Wonton noodles: A Chinese dish made with dumplings, with a variety of ingredients including: chicken, pork and vegetables, usually eaten with yellow egg noodles.

Synopsis

The Cappuccino Chronicles takes us into a world of fate, culture, modernity, friendships and family. Mala Amani is an exotic woman from India, but is not your typical '*aunty*' – a term of endearment and a pun for a woman of substance with gilded wisdom. Her two best friends Noor and Sharon illustrate how life can often take different paths and sometimes that fork in the road is for a '*bloody good reason*'.

Bazica, their home away from home, has been their coffee shop for twenty years. Sitting in the same corner almost everyday, these women reside in London, having tab after tab of cappuccinos, which help to fuel their journeys.

Each '*aunty*' has laughed, cried, and transformed at table number 8, and have sewn the pieces of their world together as friends, family, and healers to become universal agents of circumstance, perception, growth and change.

Sophia Martin is on the other side of the world and shows us how progression can sometimes stem from the unknown.

Each of these women take us on a journey by stirring up havoc, as well as delight, through a humorous outlook of our own existence on earth. The voyage of simple spirituality will whisk you away on a wave of worldly truths. These immensely multi-cultural women will compel you to travel with them around the world, as they try to find answers through signs.

Each chapter is a snapshot of these women's lives, like a photo album. As their journeys progress, their album becomes a fabric of stories interwoven into each other. Each character is forced to go through individual transformation in their search for spiritual truths which leads to self-realization, self-reflection, self-discovery and growth.

The reader will decide which woman takes on the central role, discovering that all of them will never stop learning.

About the Author

Pashmina currently lives in Asia with her family. She worked in the PR industry as an English Copywriter right after she graduated from university in London. She assisted in launching flagship stores for some big fashion companies in South East Asia. Pashmina then left the PR industry and moved on to teaching, which she has been doing for 16 years. She also recently earned her Master of Education (M.Ed) in International Teaching.

Writing is indeed her passion. Whilst at university, Pashmina wrote plays for her classmates as well as a production entitled I-N-S-O-M-N-I-A, which debuted in 1996. The second running of the play was presented again in 2001, and once again in 2008 for students at an international school.

Her family and friends, as well as her travels, are the impetus for all her imagination and creativity. She loves music, the arts and swimming in the endless ocean.

Pashmina's upcoming books include the sequel and the third book in *The Cappuccino Chronicles* series entitled *The Cappuccino Chronicles: Mocha Madness*, and *The Cappuccino Chronicles: Endless Espressos*.

Am I the One is a collection of 9 short stories about 9 families from different corners of the globe. Spiritual globalization and universal citizenship are the themes of her second book. She is also in the process of fulfilling her ultimate dream of building a reputable, state of the art theatre in Asia.

Made in the USA
Columbia, SC
21 April 2017